Window Top
Treatments

THE COMPLETE PHOTO GUIDE TO

Window Top Treatments

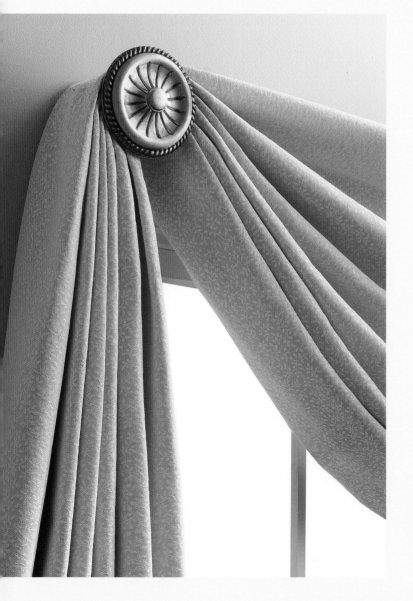

Do-It-Yourself Valances, Swags and Cornices

edited by
Linda Neubauer

Creative Publishing
international

Chanhassen, MN

Creative Publishing
international

Copyright © 2006
Creative Publishing international
18705 Lake Drive East
Chanhassen, Minnesota 55317
1-800-328-3895
www.creativepub.com
All rights reserved

President/CEO: Ken Fund
Vice President/Publisher: Linda Ball
Vice President/Retail Sales: Kevin Haas

Executive Editor: Alison Brown Cerier
Senior Editor: Linda Neubauer
Photo Stylist: Joanne Wawra
Creative Director: Brad Springer
Photographer: Steve Galvin
Production Manager: Laura Hokkanen
Text and Photo Research: Kathleen Stoehr
Cover Design: Michaelis Carpelis Design
Page Design and Layout: Lois Stanfield

Library of Congress Cataloging-in-Publication Data

   The complete photo guide to window-top treatments :
selecting, sewing, and installing valances, swags, and
cornices / edited by Linda Neubauer.
      p. cm.
   ISBN 1-58923-252-6 (soft cover)
   1. Draperies. 2. Draperies--Pictorial works. 3. Valances
(Windows)
4. Valances (Windows)--Pictorial works. I. Neubauer,
Linda. II. Title.

   TT390.S86 2006
   746.9'4--dc22

                                    2005022368

Printed in Singapore
10 9 8 7 6 5 4 3 2 1

Photography credits:
Jeff Allen, p. 11 (top), design by Donna Elle, Nantucket
Windows; Getdecorating.com, pp. 11 (right), 17 (top), 29 (top),
102; Jamie Gibbs, Jamie Gibbs & Associates, p. 99 (left);
Hunter Douglas Window Fashions, pp. 10, 80;
Interiors by Decorating Den: p. 16, design by Beverly Barrett;
p. 22, design by Wendy Ballard; p. 29 (left), design by Karen
Sanders; p. 28, design by M. Anquetil; pp. 35 (top), 40, 41
(top), 51 (top), 76, 77 (top), design by Becky Zimmerman; pp.
34, 87 (top), design by Mary Brooks; p. 35 (left), design by
Mary Gilmartin; p. 41 (right), design by Patti Hughes; p. 47,
design by Elisabeth Goldberg; pp. 46, 51 (left), 87 (bottom),
design by Rebecca Shern; pp. 50, 70, design by Lynne Lawson;
p. 54, design by Shelly Rodner; p. 55 (top), design by Joanne
Watson; p. 61 (top), design by Sally Herre; p. 60, design by
Bonnie Silbert; p. 67, design by T. Comer; p. 71 (bottom),
design by Mary Zimmerman; p. 81 (left), design by Stephanie
Clara Finkleman; pp. 86, 103 (top), design by Suzanne Price;
p. 93, design by Carolyn Jordan; p. 99 (top), design by Bonnie
Pressley; p. 103 (bottom), design by Cheryl McLean; p. 115
(top), design by Amy Noonan; p. 114 design by Connie
Thompson;
Richard Leo Johnson, p. 92 (design by Carlette Cormier, CC's
Designs); K-Blair Finials, p. 77 (bottom); Lafayette Interior
Fashions, pp. 61 (left), 66; David Duncan Livingston,
www.davidduncanlivingston.com, pp. 98, 115 (left).

Waverly decorator fabrics were used for how-to photography.
Please contact Waverly by phone, (800)423-5881, or visit their
web site, www.waverly.com.

Contents

Choosing a Style

WINDOW TOP TREATMENTS can be tailored or free-flowing, elegant or casual, simple or ornate. A top treatment can be used alone to soften the window frame and add color and style. Often, though, window top treatments are the finishing touch over curtains, draperies, shades, or blinds, where they not only embellish the look but hide clunky lift mechanisms or other hardware.

Top treatments are very popular DIY projects. They take relatively little fabric, time, or sewing experience, but add a lot of decorating style to a room.

There are many styles of top treatments, not to mention hundreds of possible fabrics and trims, so step one is deciding what you will make for the window. First, consider whether a swag, valance, or cornice is right for the room.

Swags

A swag dips in folds down into the window. The finished swag looks like one drape of fabric, though many swags are actually constructed of separate parts. Most swags have tails or other extensions on the sides. Of all window top treatments, swags are most likely to be seen alone, without curtains or shades. There are many styles of swags. While a tailored swag is crisply pleated and formal, a freeform swag looks almost windblown as it twirls across a rod or pole. Some swags are simple and informal, but others are extremely elegant. Swags are very popular in contemporary interiors.

Swags used to be made in large-scale floral prints, and most had rigid pleats. Today, swags are seen most often in flowing silks, sheers, diminutive patterns, and earth tones.

Valances

Valances, the broadest category, are top treatments of free-hanging fabric mounted on a hidden board or hung from a rod. A valance can be as simple as a flip topper, flat rectangle, or triangle; these treatments take little sewing experience and about as little time. More complex treatments in which the fabric billows and arcs are more challenging but well within reach when you follow the step-by-step directions here.

Although valances can be used alone, they are usually teamed with another treatment, such as a blind or shade or a soft drapery panel. The valance can complement the drapery underneath it with matching tones and patterns or offer a contrast.

Styles in valances have changed, too. Headings of fabric above the rod are smaller or gone. Fabric is less full or bunched on the rod. Embellishments are more common. Rods can be thick or thin, and decorative hardware is very popular.

Cornices

A cornice is made by upholstering fabric to a wooden frame. The look is structured but can be either quite casual or quite elaborate.

Cornices are often used to conceal the mechanisms of other window treatments. They can also solve problems like adjoining windows at different heights, by concealing the true top of the window. They can make a window appear lower or higher than it really is.

The most common cornice is a padded, fabric-covered rectangular box that extends about one-fifth down the window. It can have a straight or shaped lower edge and is often dressed up with decorative welting, tassels, or trims.

A little less rigid, a soft cornice is padded fabric attached to a mounting board in panels that hang down in unique shapes. It can be single or multi-layered and have scalloped edges, triangle points, graceful swoops, or whatever design you wish.

How to Use This Book

HERE ARE INSTRUCTIONS for the twenty swags, valances, and cornices that are most popular today, offering a wide range of looks and design options. Photographs show each style in a variety of room settings, décor styles, fabrics, embellishments, and hardware. You will see how decorators have approached both common window shapes and sizes and "problem windows" like those in a corner or bay.

Once you have chosen a top-treatment style, the step-by-step instructions will tell and show you how to construct it from beginning to end: measuring, cutting, sewing, even installing. It is a good idea to read all the directions before you start. The section called "what you need to know" will help with the planning; it covers information like what size to make the treatment, what type of fabric to use, and how and where to mount the finished treatment.

Also before you start, read through the basics section at the back of the book. Its insights and tips will help you get professional results with ease. You may not be familiar with some of the special terms used for window treatments, so these are explained in "terms to know" at the back of the book. The terms appear in italics the first time they come up in a project.

Materials

Each project has a materials list of everything you'll probably have to buy. The list doesn't tell you how much fabric to buy because that depends on the size of the window. The materials list assumes you have on hand basic sewing supplies. You will need pins, fabric shears, steel tape measure, carpenter's square for marking straight cutting lines, fabric

marking pens or pencils, sewing machine and attachments, thread, an iron, and a pressing surface.

Cornices

Many window top treatments are made from large rectangles of fabric that are cut straight across the fabric, with the length running parallel to the selvages. If the width needed is more than the width of the decorator fabric [usually 54" (137 cm)], two or more pieces are sewn together. Cutting directions are often set apart in a project to help you find the cut length of each piece and the total cut width. You simply multiply the cut length by the number of fabric widths needed to determine the amount of fabric to buy. Sometimes you have to draw a detailed diagram or make a pattern to find out how much fabric to buy and how to cut it. For those projects, the cutting directions are integrated into the first few steps and you have to complete them before you go shopping.

Enjoy creating just the right top treatment for your home!

Freeform Scarf Swags

A FREEFORM SCARF is an uninhibited spirit, draping effortlessly across a window frame and softening edges. A full-width, unshaped length of fabric, a freeform scarf can be sewn up in minutes. Depending on the fabric, the swag can be simple or elegant. You can choose to hang the treatment from either a decorative rod or wall-mounted swag holders.

Sheer on sheers (opposite)
This is the freeform scarf at its most elegant. It tops fabric/vane combination shades that look like sheer draperies when open and provide total privacy when closed. The swag's hemmed ends taper in gentle cascades to an elegant length just above the deep baseboard trim. Swags with such ample fullness can be sewn from extra-wide sheer fabric.

Royal treatment (above)
Deep eggplant purple velvet draws the eye upward and provides a striking contrast to the light green walls. The delicate glass-bead trim is simply draped along the lower edge—no need to stitch it on. Without this top treatment, the sheer draperies would have disappeared into the window frame, leaving an unnoticed corner of the room.

Unifying design (right)
Windows of two different heights are unified by a graceful freeform scarf swag. The swag also echoes the vaulted ceiling. It enhances rather than blocks it.

What you need to know

You can **design** scarf swags with single or multiple swoops. For a formal look, plan the swag tails to break at or puddle on the floor. The sides of shorter, less formal scarf swags can fall to the same or different lengths, to the bottom of the window or to two-thirds or one-third the window length. Large, loose knots of fabric can be worked in at the upper corners or between swoops.

Lightweight, drapable **fabric** works best for scarf swags. If the fabric has neat narrow selvages, they can be used as the finished edges, eliminating the need to sew or fuse lengthy side hems. Reversible fabrics, such as sheers and many yarn-dyed solid-color fabrics, are recommended for short swags because you will catch glimpses of the wrong side at the inner edges of the tails. If you want to use a patterned fabric, avoid fabric with a one-way design, as the design will be upside down on one side of the window.

A scarf swag can be **mounted** on swag holders of various styles or on a decorative rod. If using swag holders, mount one at each side of the window, just above the window frame and even with the frame sides. If the swag has multiple swoops, mount an additional holder for each swoop. If using a rod, mount it just above the frame with the outer brackets even with the sides. It takes a bit of practice and patience to drape scarf swags the way you want them to look. Fanfolding the entire length of the swag beforehand makes styling easier.

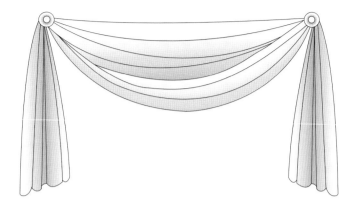

Materials

- Swag holders or decorative rod and brackets
- Tools and hardware for installation
- String
- Lightweight, drapable fabric, length determined in step 4
- Velcro strap or twill tape for bundling fabric and securing to holders or rod
- Safety pins
- Double-sided carpet tape, for securing swag to window frame or rod, optional

Making a single swag

1 Mount the swag holders or decorative rod. Drape a length of string over the rod or holders, following the line you want on the upper edge of the finished swag. (It may stretch straight across the top of the window or dip slightly.) Continue the string to the desired finished lengths at the sides. This will be the finished length on the upper edge of the swag.

2 Drape a second string over the rod or holders, dipping to the lowest points for the centers of the swags and falling to the desired finished lengths

at the sides. This will be the finished length of the lower edge of the swag. Mark both strings where they touch the pole or swag holders.

3 Measure and write down the lengths of the strings for each section. Measure the lengths shown on the diagram: 1 is from the long left point to the holder; 2 is from the long right point to the holder; 3 is the distance across the pole or between holders; and 4 is the length of the swoop between holders.

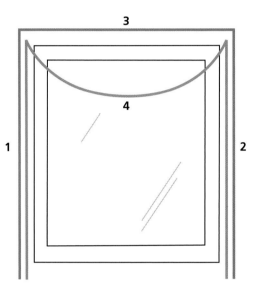

4 You will use the full width of the fabric. To find the *cut length* of the fabric, add measurements 1, 2, and 4 plus 2" (5 cm) for hems. For ends that puddle on the floor, add 15" (38 cm) for each puddle; for ends that just break at the floor, add 4" (10 cm) for each break.

5 If the selvages are neat and inconspicuous, the long edges do not need to be finished. Otherwise, trim off the selvages evenly, and turn under and stitch ½" (1.3 cm) double-fold hems on the long edges. Turn under and stitch ½" (1.3 cm) double-fold hems on the ends of the fabric length.

(continued)

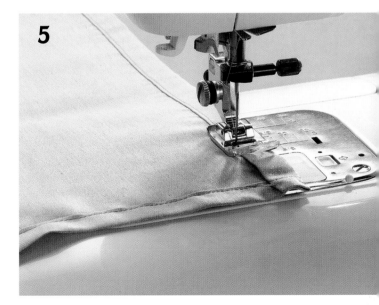

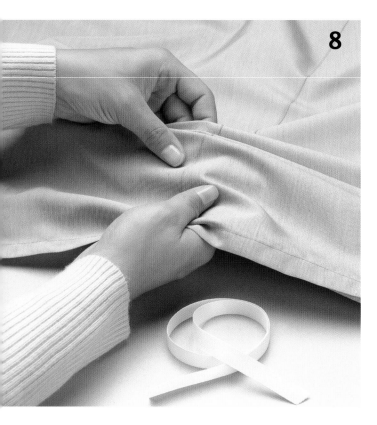

8

6 Measure from the left end of the fabric a distance equal to measurement 1; mark both selvages with a small safety pin. Repeat from the right end, measuring a distance equal to 2.

7 Subtract measurement 3 from 4; divide the result in half. Mark points on the upper edge of the center section this distance inward from the marks made in step 6. (The distance between points should equal measurement 3.) Draw light diagonal pencil or chalk lines from these points to the pin marks on the lower selvage.

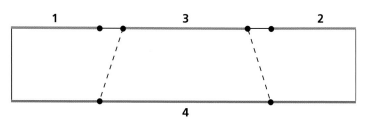

8 Fanfold the swag along the marked lines, keeping the number and depth of folds consistent; secure with a Velcro strap or twill tape.

9 Hang the swag over the rod or holders; tie or safety-pin it in place inconspicuously. If you want a straight upper edge, secure it to the rod or window frame with double-sided carpet tape.

10 Arrange the folds in the swag and down the sides. For ends that puddle on the floor, bundle and tie the swag end, flip it under, and arrange the swag around the bundle.

9

Making a swag with multiple swoops

1 Mount the hardware and drape two strings. If the swoops are evenly spaced and of equal depth, write down one measurement along the upper edge of the swoops and another measurement as the combined total of all the lower edges. Subtract the upper length from the lower length and divide the difference among the swoops; mark the upper and lower edges. If the swoops are spaced differently or are of different depths (diagram), take separate measurements for each swoop and mark as shown.

2 Mark the diagonal lines as in step 7 opposite. Fanfold and tie as in step 8. Hang and style the swag.

Making a swag with a knot

1 Mount the hardware and drape two strings as for single or multiple swoops. Allow 14" (35.5 cm) for each knot when calculating the total length of the fabric.

2 Determine the differences between the upper and lower edges. Mark light pencil lines across the fabric, leaving 14" (35.5 cm) spaces between lines if the swoops will be separated by a knot.

3 Fanfold along each marked line, keeping the number and depth of folds consistent; secure the folded bundles with Velcro straps or twill tape.

4 Tie the fabric between bundles into a large, loose knot over the rod or swag holder. Pin the bundles together inside the knot. If the treatment has multiple knots, begin in the center and work out toward each side.

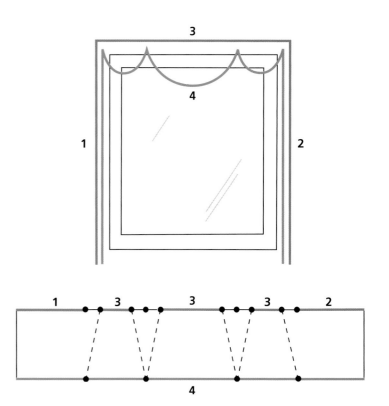

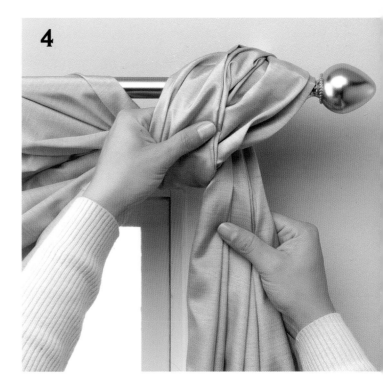

Bias Swags

A BIAS SWAG drapes in smooth, graceful folds. The fabric falls that way because it is cut with the true *bias* running through the center of the swag. Bias swags work particularly well in rooms with high ceilings. The drooping folds draw the eye from the top of the window down and then back up again.

The bias swag can look light and airy when made in semisheer fabric accented in beads that catch the light. For a traditional look, make a bias swag in medium-weight patterned fabric and trim with bullion fringe. A single swag for a small window is a lovely top treatment and easy to make. Even multiple bias swags are easy to construct because you make each swag individually and simply overlap them as you mount them.

Clever stripes (opposite)
The striped fabric in these swags, gently folding at an angle, was obviously cut on the bias. Draped well below the heading over tie tab curtains, the swags hide the gap between the top of the window and the decorative rod. The stripes are echoed in the upholstered cushions of the dining chairs, pulling the overall room design together.

Rich style (above)
The deep folds of these elegant bias swags, accented with long bullion fringe, are the perfect choice for this high-style interior. The majestic swag holders look like the tops of ancient columns.

Rings (left)
Overlapped at the center, these white satin bias swags are attached to a decorator pole with clip-on rings. The rings (which could also be sewn on) are an unexpected touch for a swag treatment.

17

What you need to know

Design this top treatment as a single swag or overlapping multiple swags. The pattern for the swag is made from one-fourth of a circle. The instructions that follow are based on a circle with a 42" (107 cm) radius and result in a swag that is 36" (91.5 cm) wide and 20" (51 cm) long at the center. Swags sewn this size can be a few inches narrower and longer or wider and shorter by varying the spacing between the rings on the pole. For larger swags, begin with a larger circle.

Make a swag with a soft, airy look, using semisheer decorator **fabric** for the outer fabric and the *lining*. For a more formal, traditional look, the swag can be made from a medium-weight decorator fabric and trimmed with a bullion fringe along the curved edges. Bias swags made from striped or plaid fabric can be very interesting.

To **mount** the swags, attach either clip-on or sew-on rings to the upper edge and slide the rings onto a decorator pole. To keep the rings from shifting, apply a small amount of floral adhesive clay or poster putty to the inside of each ring along the top. Hang swags over a traversing *undertreatment* on a rod with a deep enough *projection* to keep the swags from rubbing against the undertreatment as it moves. If the undertreatment is mounted on a utility rod, mount the pole for the swags high enough to hide the undertreatment's upper edge. Bias swags can also be mounted on the same rod as a stationary undertreatment.

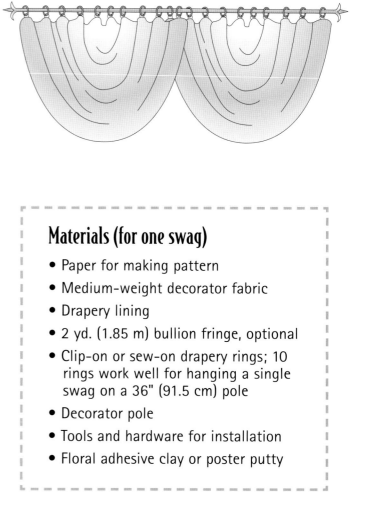

Materials (for one swag)

- Paper for making pattern
- Medium-weight decorator fabric
- Drapery lining
- 2 yd. (1.85 m) bullion fringe, optional
- Clip-on or sew-on drapery rings; 10 rings work well for hanging a single swag on a 36" (91.5 cm) pole
- Decorator pole
- Tools and hardware for installation
- Floral adhesive clay or poster putty

Making a pattern

1 Cut a 42" (107 cm) square of paper; fold it in half diagonally. Using a straightedge and pencil, draw an arc between the square corner and the fold, marking the lower edge of the swag. Cut on the marked line through both layers.

2 Mark the folded edge 5" (12.7 cm) from the upper point. Draw a line from the mark to the opposite edges, perpendicular to the fold. Cut on the marked line.

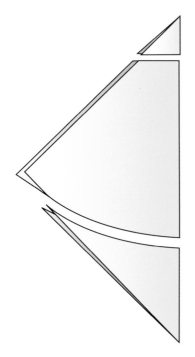

3 Fold under 2" (5 cm) on the long straight edges. At the lower edge, trim the area that is folded under, following the curve. Unfold the pattern.

(continued)

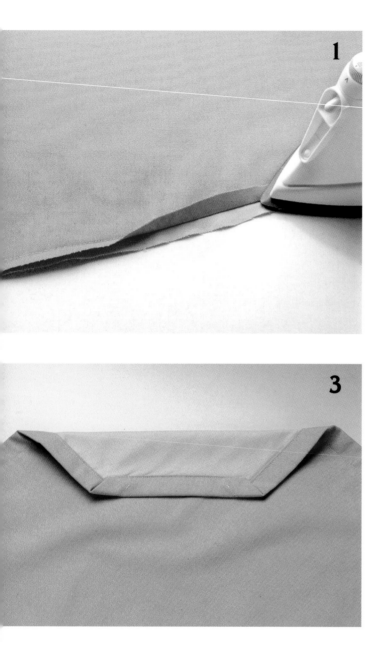

Cutting directions

- Cut one piece of decorator fabric and one piece of *lining*, using the pattern drawn on page 19. Align the straight edges of the pattern to the *lengthwise* and *crosswise grains* of the fabric. If you are cutting more than one swag, cut a single layer at a time for the most efficient use of the fabric.

Making a bias swag

1 Pin the decorator fabric and lining right sides together, along the curved edge. Stitch a ½" (1.3 cm) seam; press the seam allowances open.

2 Turn the swag right side out. Press the curved edge.

3 Press under 1" (2.5 cm) twice on the long straight sides, folding the decorator fabric and lining together. Stitch close to the inner fold. Repeat at the upper edge. Apply fringe to the curved edge if desired.

4 Attach 10 drapery rings to the upper straight edges of the swag, positioning one ring at each end, one at each corner, and the remaining six rings evenly spaced between the ends and corners.

5 Hang the rings on a mounted decorator pole. Arrange the swag to the desired width and length. Arrange the swag into four deep, curving folds, pulling the fabric forward between rings. Pull the fabric between the center two rings forward.

6 Apply floral adhesive clay or poster putty to the inside of the rings, along the top, if necessary to keep the rings from shifting.

Overlapping swags

7 Atttach 18 rings to the upper straight edges of the swags as in step 4, opposite, overlapping the swags by one fold width, so the two center rings are attached to both swags.

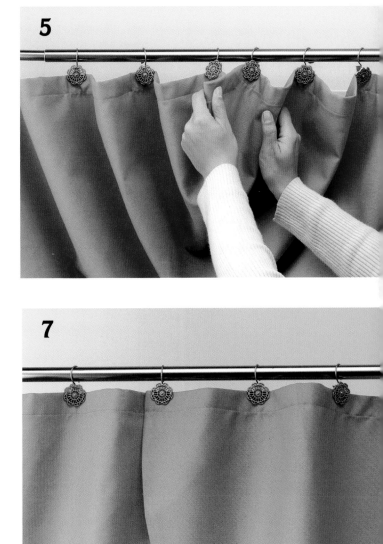

Tapered Scarf Swags

TAPERED SCARF SWAGS look like freeform scarf swags (page 10), but have a more precise drape with smooth, even folds and are lined for extra body. Used alone to punctuate the top of a window or as a complement to draperies or blinds, the versatile tapered scarf swag is suited for many décor styles. Depending on the fabric and hardware chosen, as well as the length of the tails, a tapered scarf can work in rooms as varied as a breakfast nook and a stately living room.

Peaked arch (opposite)
Wide, arched windows can be a tricky situation. This tapered scarf swag with multiple swoops that rise to a peak over a living room window pulls the window together. The dramatic treatment draws attention to the window without impeding the view. Decorative fringe and swag holders complete the look.

Simple elegance (top right)
Cotton jacquard decorator fabric turned infinitely elegant. Wedges cut from the fabric during construction allow effortless draping of the tapered scarf over holders into precise folds.

Casual print (bottom right)
Floral print fabric was draped through scarf rings to form this easy single swoop treatment. Because there are hidden seams at the points where the swag goes through the rings, a directional print like this can run upward on both tails.

*W*hat you need to know

Design swags that drape into a single swoop or into multiple swoops. The tails can stop just short of, break at, or puddle on the floor (the last is most formal). Shorter tails that come to the bottom of the window frame or to points two-thirds or one-third the window length have ends that angle up and in toward the window. In this method, the shaping of the swag is achieved by cutting wedges of excess *fullness* from a length of fabric at each point where the swag crosses a swag holder or pole. The swag is then constructed by sewing the angled pieces together and adding a *lining*.

This scarf swag uses the full width of the **fabric** and can be either self-lined or lined in a contrasting fabric. Nearly any decorator fabric can be used, from semisheer to brocade. Even one-way prints are suitable, because the direction of the fabric can be switched at a tail seam.

Holders for **mounting** the swags are available in several styles, including medallions and scarf rings; decorative tieback holders and holdbacks can also be used. A tapered swag with a single swoop can also be draped over a decorative pole. Mount the holders at the upper corners of the window frame and in any other desired locations before beginning the project, and measure for the treatment using twill tape.

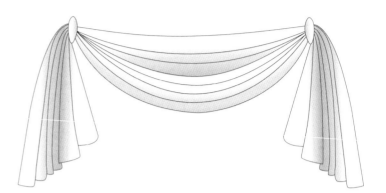

Materials

- Decorative swag holders (one holder at each upper corner of the window for a swag with a single swoop, and one holder for each additional swoop) or decorative pole
- Tools and hardware for installation
- Twill tape
- Decorator fabric for swag, length determined in step 1, page 24 for swag with single swoop or step 1, page 26 for swag with multiple swoops
- Matching or contrasting fabric for lining, length equal to decorator fabric
- Double-sided carpet tape, optional

Measuring for a single swoop

1 Mount the swag holders or decorative pole in the desired locations. Drape a length of twill tape over the holders or pole, extending to the desired length of the sides and stretching straight across the top of the window. This will be the finished length of the top and outer sides of the swag.

2 Drape a second length of twill tape over the holders or pole, extending to the desired

shortest points of the tapered sides and dipping to the lowest point desired at the center of the swoop. This will be the finished length of the bottom and inner sides of the swag. Mark both tapes at the holders or outermost points on the pole.

3 Measure and record the lengths of the tape for each section. Measurement 1 is from the long point to the holder or pole, 2 is from the short point to the holder or pole, 3 is the distance straight across between the holders or along the pole, and 4 is the length of the lower edge of the swoop.

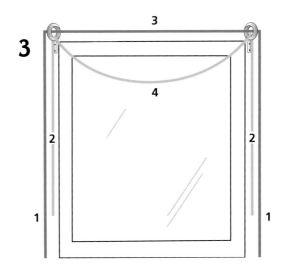

Sewing a single swoop

4 Cut the full width of the fabric, with the length equal to measurement 4 plus two times measurement 1 plus 3" (7.5 cm) for seam allowances. Measure from each end of the fabric a distance equal to 1 plus 1" (2.5 cm). Cut across the fabric perpendicular to the selvages at these points, to separate the end pieces from the center.

5 Turn one end piece completely around, if the fabric has a one-way design, so the upward direction on both ends points to the middle; when hung, the design will face in the correct direction on both ends. Label the top of each end piece.

6 Subtract measurement 2 from measurement 1. Mark a point on the inner edge of one end piece this distance from the lower cut edge. Draw a line from this point to the lower outside corner; cut away the triangular wedge. Repeat for the other end piece, cutting the angle in the opposite direction.

7 Subtract measurement 3 from measurement 4; divide this measurement in half. Mark a point on the top edge of the center piece this distance from one cut end. Draw a line from this point

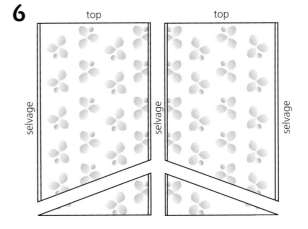

(continued)

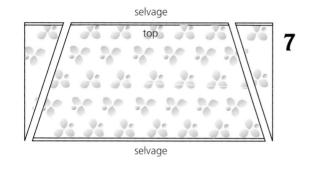

7

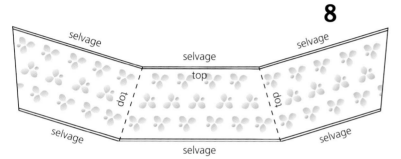

8

10

to the lower corner; cut away the triangular wedge. Repeat for the opposite cut end of the center piece.

8 Trim off the selvages. Cut the lining, using the swag pieces as patterns; label the tops of the lining pieces. Stitch the swag pieces together using 1/2" (1.3 cm) seams, easing the edges to fit; repeat for the lining pieces. Press the seam allowances open.

9 Pin the lining to the swag, right sides together. Stitch a 1/2" (1.3 cm) seam all around, leaving an opening along the center top for turning. Trim the corners diagonally. Press the lining seam allowance toward the lining.

10 Turn the swag right side out; press the seamed edges. Slipstitch the opening closed. Fanfold the swag along the seam lines, keeping the number and depth of folds consistent. Tie the folds with twill tape. Hang the swag through scarf rings or over medallion-style scarf holders or tieback holders. Or hang the swag over a pole, with the center swoop in front. Arrange the folds in the swag and sides. Remove the twill tape. If necessary, secure the fabric to the holder or pole inconspicuously, using double-sided carpet tape.

Measuring for multiple swoops

1 Mount the swag holders or pole in the desired locations. Drape a length of twill tape over the holders or pole, extending to the longest points of the tapered sides and stretching straight across the top of the window or pole. This will be the finished length of the top of the swag.

2 Drape a second length of twill tape over the holders or pole, extending to the shortest points of the tapered sides and dipping to the lowest point desired at the center of each swoop. This

will be the finished length on the bottom of the swag. Mark both tapes at the holders or at the attachment points on the pole.

3 Measure and record the lengths of the tape for each section. Measurement 1 is from the long point to the holder or pole. Measurement 2 is from the short point to the holder or pole. Measurement 3 is the distance straight across between the holders or along the pole. Measurement 4 is the total length of all the swoops between the end holders or end attachment points to the pole.

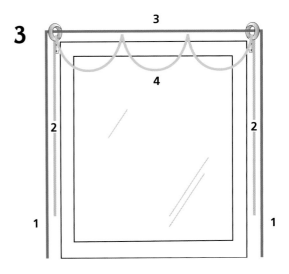

Sewing multiple swoops

4 Cut the full width of the fabric, with the length equal to measurement 4 plus two times measurement 1 plus 1" (2.5 cm) for each swoop plus an additional 2" (5 cm). Measure from each end of the fabric a distance equal to measurement 1 plus 1" (2.5 cm). Cut across the fabric perpendicular to the selvages at these points. Follow steps 5 and 6 on page 25.

5 Measure the length of the center piece; divide this measurement by the number of swoops in the swag. Mark the center piece into lengths of this size; cut the fabric perpendicular to the selvages at these points.

6 Subtract measurement 3 from measurement 4. Divide this measurement by the number of swoops in the swag; then divide this number in half. Mark a point on the top edge of one swoop piece this distance from one cut end. Draw a line from this point to the lower corner; cut away the triangular wedge. Repeat for the opposite cut end of the same piece. Cut identical wedges from each remaining swoop piece. Complete the swag as in steps 8 to 10, opposite.

Tailored Swags

DIFFERENT FROM SCARF swags, the tailored version of this popular top treatment is more structured and has a formal pleated look. It is not formed at the window, but rather created with a muslin pattern to fit the window perfectly. This treatment is often designed in lavish layers of multiple, overlapping swags and coupled with floor-length pleated panels at the ends or with jabots (page 34) at the ends and between swags. Though they may appear to be a long sweep of fabric simply draped over a rod or board, in fact each swag and any side pieces are made separately and invisibly attached with staples or hook-and-loop tape. In traditional interiors, the jabots are usually placed behind the swag. Placing the tails in front makes the window appear narrower and taller.

Layers of swags (opposite)
Swags in alternating earth tones create drama but also softness for a master bedroom. The sheer, deep swag hung in back echoes the arched side window.

Traditional arrangement (top)
This opulent swag in rich red is board-mounted over full-length stationary side panels.

Many pieces (left)
Each piece of this treatment was made and attached separately. The lustrous ivory stripe fabric of the top swags was used to line the jabots, unifying the look.

*W*hat you need to know

Design your treatment with one swag or many, depending on the width of the window and your preference. Each swag should be no wider than 40" (102 cm). This size can be adapted to any window size by increasing or decreasing the overlapping of adjoining swags. A swag is usually 15" to 20" (38 to 51 cm) long at the longest point in the center. Shallower swags may be used on narrow windows.

Make the swag pattern from muslin or an old sheet that will drape softly. Drape the muslin and pin it at different positions until you find the look you like. For each swag, you will need 1 yd. (.95 m) of decorator **fabric** and *lining* if the draped tape measurement (step 1) is less than the fabric width; you will need 2 yd. (1.85 m) if the draped measurement is more than the fabric width.

Mount the swags to a cornice, mounting board, or decorative pole placed 4" (10 cm) above the molding if used alone, or about 4" (10 cm) above the drapery rod if used over draperies. The board or pole *return* must be deep enough to clear the underdrapery. In homes with beautiful moldings the swags may be mounted inside the window on a board that fits inside the frame, and there are no returns.

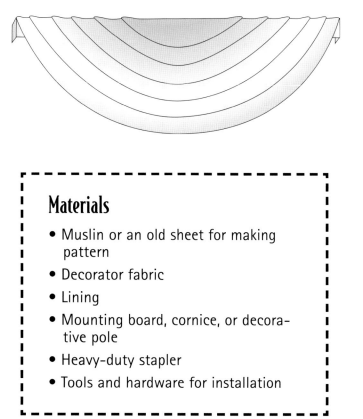

Materials

- Muslin or an old sheet for making pattern
- Decorator fabric
- Lining
- Mounting board, cornice, or decorative pole
- Heavy-duty stapler
- Tools and hardware for installation

Making the pattern

1 Drape a string to simulate the planned shape of the swag. For double swags, drape two strings. If the swag will go under the jabots, it usually

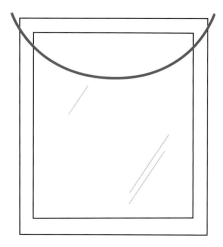

extends to within 2" (5 cm) of the ends of the mounting board.

2 Cut muslin for the swag pattern 36" (91.5 cm) long with the cut width equal to the measurement of the draped string plus 4" (10 cm). Draw a line 1" (2.5 cm) from the upper edge, and mark the desired finished width of the swag centered on the line. Centered on the lower edge, mark the measured length of the string. Connect the marks, forming diagonal guidelines. Divide each guideline equally into one more space than the number of folds; mark. For example, for five folds, divide each line into six spaces.

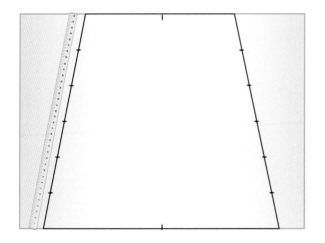

3 Pin the upper edge of the muslin to a padded surface, such as an ironing board, with the marked line along the front edge. Fold the muslin on the first mark of the diagonal line, and raise the fold to the top line, about 5" (12.7 cm) from the end; pin. Repeat on the opposite side.

4 Fold the muslin on the second mark of the diagonal line, and raise the fold to the top line, ½" (1.3 cm) outside the first fold. Repeat on the opposite side. Continue pinning the folds in place along the upper marked line.

(continued)

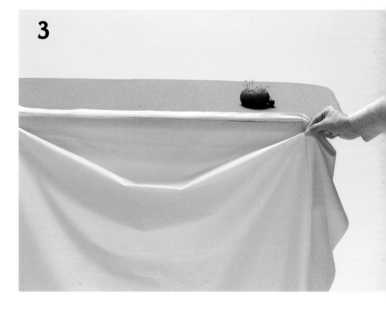

3

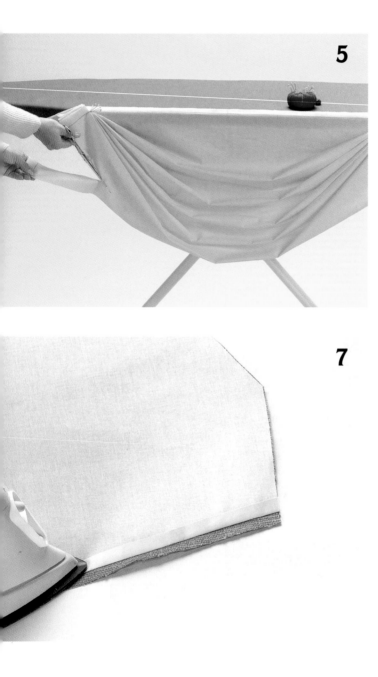

5 Adjust the pins and folds as necessary to achieve the desired appearance. Trim the excess fabric straight across, 1" (2.5 cm) from the upper edges. Trim the outer edge to about 3" (7.5 cm) from the last fold.

6 Unpin the folds. Fold the pattern in half lengthwise to check that the sides match; adjust the cutting lines as necessary. Use the pattern to cut the swag and lining. Add ½" (1.3 cm) seam allowance on the lower edge.

Making a Tailored Swag

7 Pin the lining to the swag, right sides together, along the lower curved edge. Stitch the curved edge in a ½" (1.3 cm) seam. Press the lining seam allowance toward the lining. Turn the swag right side out; press the stitched edge.

8 Pin the swag front and lining together along the open edges. *Finish* the edges together by serging or zigzag stitching.

9 Fold the swag at the notch points and pin the folds in place along the upper edge, just as they were arranged when you made the pattern. Pin the upper edge of the swag to a padded surface to check the way it drapes. Make minor adjustments as needed. Remove the swag from the padded surface, keeping the folds pinned in place.

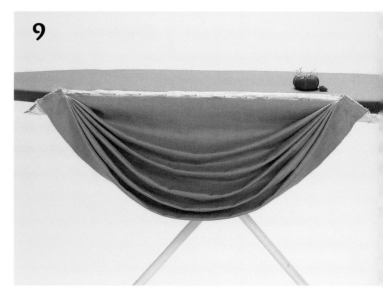

10 Stitch across all the folds at the upper edge.

11 Cut the mounting board to the correct length. Secure angle irons to the bottom of the mounting board, near the ends and at 45" (115 cm) intervals, using pan-head screws. Mount the board (page 123), centered above the window frame. Remove the screws that hold the mounting board to the angle irons, leaving the angle irons on the wall.

12 Center the swag on the mounting board with the edge of the swag 1" (2.5 cm) from the front edge of the board. Staple the swag to the board at 6" (15 cm) intervals.

13 Mount the swag by reattaching the board to the angle irons.

Jabots

THE JABOT (also known as a tail or cascade) is a decorative fabric drop that adds interest and beauty to a tailored swag treatment. It can be sleekly pleated or softly gathered, simple or ornately trimmed. Though a jabot sometimes looks like an extension or tail of the swag, it is a separate lined panel of fabric that is attached over or under the board-mounted or pole-mounted swag. Typically, jabots taper to a point, revealing a contrasting lining at the inner edge. A jabot is a vertical element that can visually balance the horizontal swag.

Walls of windows (opposite)
A long treatment of swags and jabots stretches across all these windows, tying them together while letting in lots of sunlight. The short contrasting jabots are made from shaped and pleated cylinders of fabric. Decorative hardware medallions add an elegant touch.

Corner treatment (top right)
Tailored board-mounted swags with jabots in pristine white transform the corner of this dining room. Each asymmetrical treatment has the jabot in the corner. Plump Chinese ball knots add emphasis.

Odd numbers (left)
This photo shows part of a single treatment that spans two identical windows (another swag and long jabot complete the right side). In the design of window treatments, odd-numbered combinations (three, five, etc.) are best. Notice how this treatment was designed in combinations of five: five pleats on the shorter and longer jabots, as well as five swag folds. Coordinating tassels were added.

$\mathcal{W}$hat you need to know

Jabots can be **designed** in many styles, though most often they are knife-pleated with pleats turned outward. Jabots on the sides of the window are 9" to 11" (23 to 28 cm) wide and taper upward on the inner edge, revealing the contrasting *lining* on the underside of the pleats. Side jabots are usually mirror images of each other, though they can be different lengths to create asymmetrical effects. The jabot length should be about one-third of the drapery or window length, or should fall to the sill or floor. Its shortest inner point should be lower than the center of the swag. Jabots between swags taper upward from a center long point, which is usually shorter than jabots on the sides of the treatment. Jabots are also made in a variety of shapes resembling neckties or flared fabric cylinders. Some can be fashioned from simple squares, rectangles, or wedges of fabric that are *lined-to-the-edge*. Other jabots, such as the pleated cylinder shown on page 34, are created from a pattern.

Fabric used for the jabots in a treatment should be the same as the fabric used for the swags, if you want to create the illusion that they are one continuous piece. The lining should be a decorator fabric, either the same as the face fabric or a contrasting color.

Jabots are **mounted** to the board or pole either under or over the swag at the outer edges of the window treatment or between multiple swags in a treatment. When the treatment is mounted on a board or cornice, the jabot has *returns* that cover the ends of the cornice or mounting board.

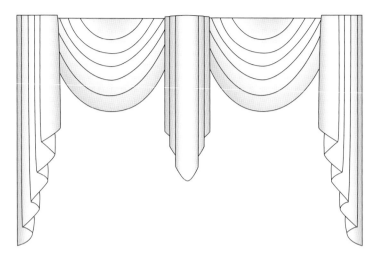

Making side jabots

1 Cut muslin for the jabot pattern three times the finished width plus the return depth plus 1" (2.5 cm) for seam allowances. Cut the length 1½" (3.8 cm) longer than the desired finished length at the return. Mark a point on the lower edge the depth of the return plus ½" (1.3 cm). On the side opposite the return, mark the vertical edge 1½" (3.8 cm) longer than the desired shortest point. Connect the marks in a diagonal line. Cut out the pattern for the jabot.

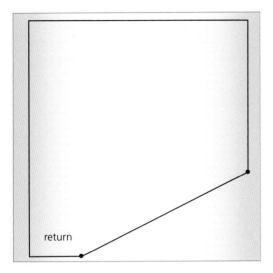

return

2 Place the jabot fabric and lining fabric right sides together. Cut out the jabot, using the pattern. Remove the pattern. Pin the layers together around the outer edge. Repeat for the jabot on the other side of the treatment, but flip the pattern so the jabots are mirror images (taper in opposite directions).

3 Stitch 1/2" (1.3 cm) seams on the sides and bottom. Trim the corners diagonally. Press the lining seam allowance away from the lining. Turn the jabot right side out and press. Repeat for the other jabot.

4 *Finish* the upper edges together by serging or zigzag stitching. Lay a jabot, lining side up, on a pressing surface. Fold under the long side the depth of the return and press the fold.

5 Turn the jabot right side up. Fold the jabot into evenly spaced pleats and press lightly. Pin the pleats along the upper edge. Stitch 1/2" (1.3 cm) from the upper edge to hold the pleats in place.

6 Repeat steps 4 and 5 for the other jabot, making sure the pleats are equal in size.

(continued)

5

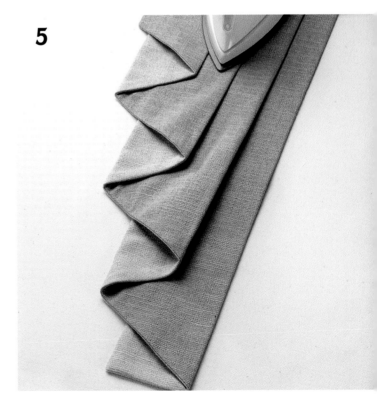

7 Staple the swag to the board (page 33), if the jabots will go over the swag. Place the top of one jabot at the end of the mounting board, with the upper edge 1" (2.5 cm) from the edge of the board and the pressed fold at the corner. Staple the return edge to the board. Position the pleats on the mounting board over the swag. Miter excess fabric at the corner and staple in place. Repeat for the second jabot. Or secure the jabots first and then staple the swag over them.

Making inner jabots

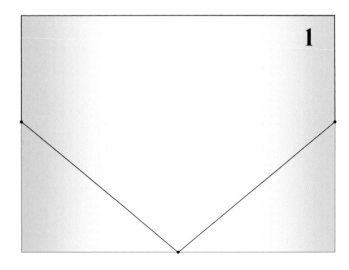

1 Cut muslin for the jabot pattern three times the finished width plus 1" (2.5 cm) for seam allowances. Cut the length 1½" (3.8 cm) longer than the desired finished length at the center. Mark a point at the center of the lower edge. Draw the vertical outer edges 1½" (3.8 cm) longer than the desired shortest points. Connect the marks in diagonal lines. Cut out the pattern for the jabot.

2 Using the pattern, cut one jabot and one lining piece. Place the jabot and lining right sides together. Stitch ½" (1.3 cm) seams on the sides and tapered lowered edge, pivoting at the center point on the bottom. Trim the corners diagonally. Press the lining seam allowance away from the lining. Turn the jabot right side out and press.

3 Finish the upper edges together by serging or zigzag stitching. Working from the center outward, fold the jabot into evenly spaced pleats and press lightly. There will be a box pleat at the center and knife pleats that point toward the outer edges. Pin the pleats along the upper edge. Stitch ½" (1.3 cm) from the upper edge to hold the pleats in place.

4 Staple the swag to the board (page 33). Staple the jabots to the mounting board, centered over the points where the swags meet.

Making cylinder jabots

1 Enlarge the pattern to the desired size and cut it out. For each jabot, cut two mirror-image pieces of the same fabric or of two contrasting fabrics (outer fabric and lining), using the pattern.

2 Align the straight outer edges of one piece, right sides together, and stitch a ½" (1.3 cm) seam, forming a cone. Press the seam allowances open. Repeat for the lining.

3 Pin the outer fabric and lining right sides together along the lower flared edge. Stitch a ¼" (6 mm) seam, pivoting at the point. Turn the jabot right side out and press the lower edge.

4 Align the upper edges of the outer fabric and lining and finish them together by serging or zigzag stitching.

5 Fold the jabot along the fold lines, including the long seam sewn in step 2. Press lightly. Baste across the top to hold the pleats in place. Staple the jabot in place over the swags.

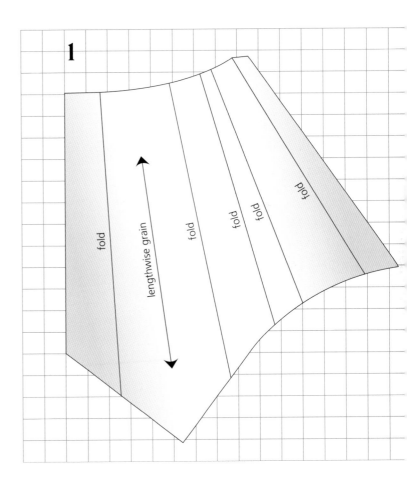

39

Flip Toppers

FLAT FABRIC PANELS that flip over decorative rods are very easy to make, yet so many creative designs are possible. These toppers are simply *lined-to-the-edge* panels made with two contrasting or coordinating fabrics. The edges are often fringed, beaded, or banded. The panels can come to a point or other shape. For added interest, the topper can be secured with buttons or grommets with ties, though they usually stay in place just by flipping them over the rod.

Asian inspiration (opposite)
Bright botanical prints pop against the black background of this elegant, Asian-inspired treatment. Several individual flip toppers, including long end panels, were hung over a decorative rod at various heights.

Layers (above)
Three thin flip toppers that look like elegant bell pulls accented with gorgeous red and gold tassels are layered over a straight flip topper panel, turning a small library window into a focal point.

Triple bay (right)
Three triangle-point flip toppers mounted on pressure rods accentuate a bay window in this dining room. In each, you see the floral print of the top layer and the plain fabric of the lining. Fringe is silhouetted against the glass.

What you need to know

Because you first create a paper pattern, you can **design** your flip topper with straight, curved, or pointed lower edges—any shape imaginable. Sometimes a printed fabric design will offer inspiration for the topper shape.

Medium-weight to heavyweight decorator **fabrics** can be used for flip toppers; lightweight fabrics can be used for one side if they are opaque. If your topper must be wider than the standard decorator fabric width, look for fabric with a nondirectional print that can be *railroaded* to avoid unsightly vertical seams. A layer of *interlining* is sandwiched between the front and back fabrics to add body, prevent shadowing of printed designs, and give support for any buttonholes or grommets.

Mount a decorator rod just above the window or higher on the wall if you want to create the illusion that the window is higher. If there is an *undertreatment*, the flip topper should stand at least 2" (5 cm) in front of it. The sides of the flip topper should extend slightly beyond the window frame or undertreatment; there are no *returns* on flip toppers. If mounted between kitchen cupboards or inside deep window frames, plain pressure rods can be used.

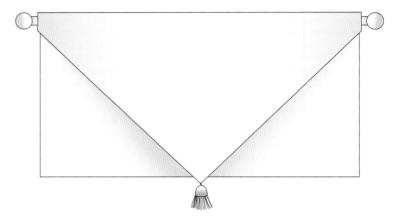

Materials

- Decorative curtain rod
- Tools and hardware for installation
- Wide kraft paper or newsprint for making pattern
- Two coordinating, firmly woven fabrics
- Drapery lining
- Paper-backed fusible adhesive, 3/8" (1 cm) wide
- Buttons or small grommets and ribbons or cording, optional

Making a flip topper

1 Mount the rod just above the window frame, with the finials extending just beyond the sides of the frame. Measure from bracket to bracket to determine the pattern width. Hang a tape measure over the rod to determine the pattern length, as shown in the diagram.

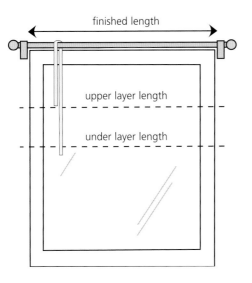

finished length

upper layer length

under layer length

2 Cut a paper pattern; shape the lower edges as desired. Hang the pattern over the rod to check the fit and shape. Draw a line where the pattern crosses the rod. Measure the total pattern length and buy equal amounts of two fabrics and lining. Preshrink all three fabrics if you intend to launder the topper.

(continued)

2

3 Pin the pattern over one of the fabrics. The outer edge of the pattern is the stitching line for the topper. Mark the cutting line on the fabric ½" (1.3 cm) beyond the pattern edge. Cut out the fabric. Remove the pattern.

4 Place the other fabric faceup over the interlining. Place the cut fabric facedown over both layers, aligning all grain lines. Pin the layers together around the edge of the cut fabric. Cut the other layers, leaving the pins in the fabric.

5 Stitch around the edge, using ½" (1.3 cm) seam allowances; leave a 10" (25.5 cm) opening for turning along one straight side. Clip the outer corners diagonally; clip up to, but not through, the stitching at inner corners and on curves.

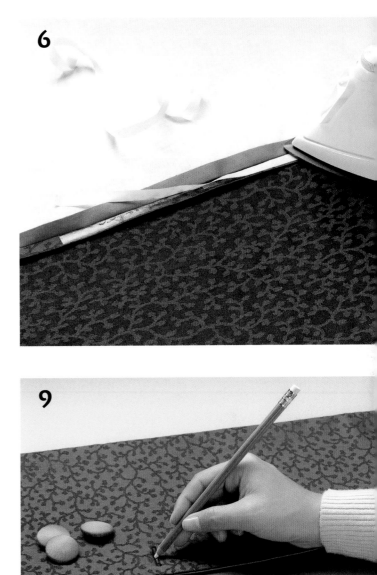

6 Press the seam allowances open. Press back the seam allowances of the opening ½" (1.3 cm). Fuse a 10" (25.5 cm) strip of fusible adhesive over the seam allowance of the opening, following the manufacturer's directions.

7 Turn the topper right side out through the opening; press. Remove the protective paper backing from the fusible adhesive strip; fuse the opening closed.

8 Fold the topper front down, using the line drawn on the pattern as a guide. If you are using buttons or grommets, mark the placement of any buttonholes or grommets. Sew buttonholes and cut them open. Or insert grommets, following the manufacturer's directions.

9 Refold the topper. Mark the placement for buttons or ties on the lower layer. Sew on buttons or ties. Flip the topper over the rod and secure.

Triangle Valances

THE TRIANGLE VALANCE, which hangs to a point like a kerchief, is casual, pretty, and easy to make. A square of decorator fabric is folded in half diagonally and stitched to make a self-lined triangle. The side points of the triangle are secured to the upper corners of the window, allowing the center to fall to a point in relaxed folds. A crystal, string of beads, or tassel can be dangled from the center point of the triangle.

Mini-triangles (opposite)
A chain of petite triangles adds a whimsical touch to a child's bedroom. Narrow ties in a smaller, coordinating plaid join the triangle corners and secure them to decorative rods with cute bows.

Straight-grain kerchief (right)
This striped triangle valance adds color and patterning to a dressing area.

What you need to know

Designing a triangle valance is easy because the size is adjustable. For instance, a valance made from a 45" (115 cm) square will fit a window width of 36" to 45" (91.5 to 115 cm) simply by pulling up more or less fabric at the upper corners. Experiment with muslin or an old sheet. As an easy guide, begin with a square the same width as the window. The wider you make the valance, the longer it will be at the center, so for very wide windows, make a continuous valance of small triangles with overlapping ends.

Any **fabric** will work, though lightweight and medium-weight fabrics that drape softly work the best. Plaids can be dynamic when turned on point this way. If the fabric tends to let light through, *interline* the valance with drapery lining.

In the directions that follow, the valance is **mounted** by pulling the ends through small rings secured to hooks at the upper corners of the window frame. Triangle valances can also be mounted by tying the corners to a decorative rod or pulling them through rings at the ends of the rod.

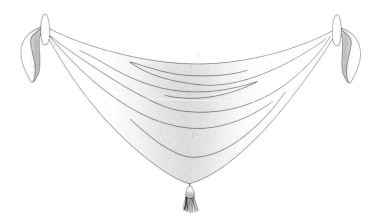

Materials

- Test fabric, such as muslin
- Decorator fabric
- Paper-backed fusible adhesive, 3/8" (1 cm) wide
- Embellishment for center point, optional
- Metal rings, 1" (2.5 cm) diameter
- Cup hooks or tieback hooks
- Tools and hardware for installation

Making a triangle valance

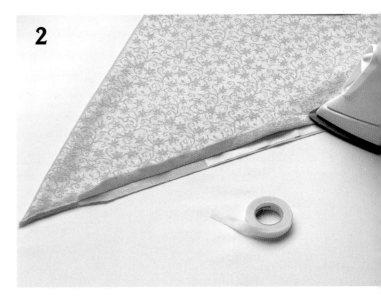

1 Cut a square of decorator fabric, using a carpenter's square to ensure right angles and equal sides. Fold the square in half diagonally, right sides together. Stitch ½" (1.3 cm) from the cut edges, leaving a 6" (15 cm) opening for turning.

2 Taper the seam allowances at the narrow points; trim diagonally across the square corner. Press the seam allowances open. Press back the seam allowances of the opening ½" (1.3 cm). Fuse a 6" (15 cm) strip of fusible adhesive over one seam allowance of the opening, following the manufacturer's directions.

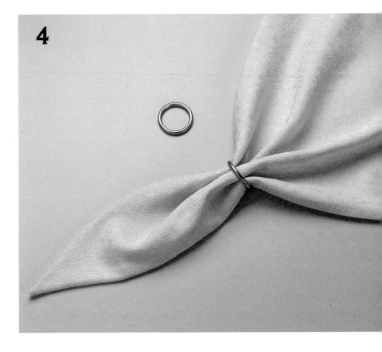

3 Turn the valance right side out through the opening; press the seamed edges. Do not press the bias fold. Remove the protective paper backing from the fusible adhesive strip; fuse the opening closed. Stitch an embellishment to the center point, if desired.

4 Insert the side points of the valance through metal rings. Test the fit by holding the valance up to the window; adjust the amount of fabric pulled through the rings, if necessary. Hand-tack the valance to the rings. Hang the rings on cup hooks or tieback hooks installed at the upper corners of the window frame.

Lined Rectangle Valances

*L*INED RECTANGLE VALANCES are simply a length of fabric *lined-to-the-edge* with the same or contrasting fabric. Many different looks can be created by changing the dimensions of the rectangle or the way the valance is hung, either clipped to a decorative rod or stapled to a mounting board. The valance can have sleek, straight lines or lots of dips and curves. The simplest version, taught in the steps that follow, is merely draped flat over a mounting board, much like a short tablecloth. Add your choice of trims to make your treatment unique: think about beaded edging, brush fringe, or tassels.

Ripples (opposite)

A long, narrow, self-lined rectangle in subtle earth tones is attached to the rod with rings at evenly spaced intervals, unifying this casual sitting area. The rippled effect is created simply by pulling the fabric forward between rings.

Quick and easy (top)

This purple rectangle valance, lined in pale blue, is accented with beads and tassels and draped from decorative finials. Though quick and easy to make, it pulls together the bathroom color scheme without overpowering the small space.

Mock swag (left)

Styled to look like a soft swag, this board-mounted lined rectangle softens this dormer window. Delicate beaded edging accents the slight curve and box-pleated corners.

What you need to know

Sketch your **design** and measure the window to plan the dimensions of the valance. In the directions that follow, a simple kerchief valance is stapled to a mounting board so the face and sides hang to the same length. The corners fall to soft rounded points. For this *self-lined* valance, a long rectangle of fabric is folded in half lengthwise and seamed on the sides and top to encase the raw edges. Thus, the same fabric forms the face of the valance as well as the *lining*. *Interlining* gives the valance more body and prevents show-through on patterned fabrics.

The right **fabric** depends on the way you intend to style your valance. Choose medium-weight, drapable fabric for a relaxed look. Choose a firmly woven fabric that is slightly stiff to create more rigid dips and curves. To avoid distracting seams in this valance, select a fabric that can be *railroaded*, such as a solid color or a print that can be turned sideways.

Plan to **mount** the board just above the window frame, 1" (2.5 cm) beyond the frame on the sides. This will allow room to install the board, using angle irons at the ends. If your valance will be hung from a rod, decide whether or not you want the window frame to show and install the rod accordingly.

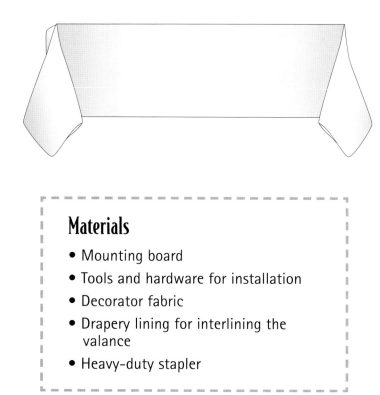

Materials

- Mounting board
- Tools and hardware for installation
- Decorator fabric
- Drapery lining for interlining the valance
- Heavy-duty stapler

Cutting directions

Railroad the fabric to eliminate the need for seams.

- The *cut length* (vertical) of the fabric equals twice the drop length plus twice the mounting board *projection* plus 1" (2.5 cm).

- The *cut width* (horizontal) of the fabric equals the length (end to end) of the mounting board plus twice the drop length of the valance plus 1" (2.5 cm).

- Cut the interlining the same width and exactly half the length of the valance fabric.

Making a lined rectangle valance

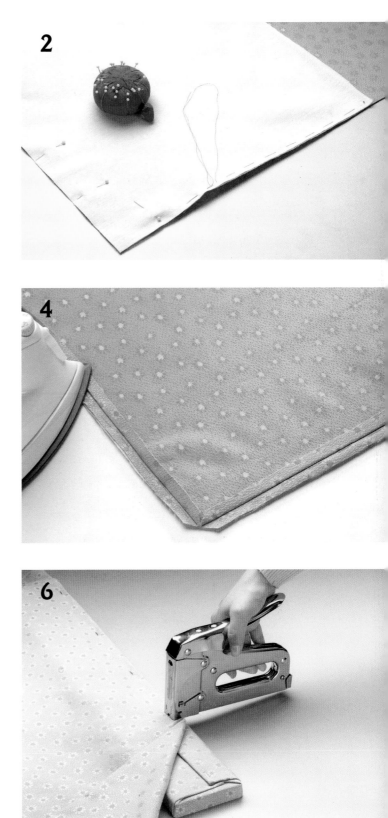

2

1 Cut the board and cover it with fabric (page 123). Mount the board (page 124), centered above the window frame. Remove the board, leaving the angle irons on the wall.

2 Place the interlining over the wrong side of the valance panel, aligning the sides and upper edge. Baste within the ½" (1.3 cm) seam allowance.

3 Fold the valance right sides together, aligning the long edges and sides. Stitch ½" (1.3 cm) seams at the ends and the upper edge. Leave an opening along the upper edge for turning the valance right side out.

4 Trim the corners diagonally to within ⅛" (3 mm) of the stitching. With the interlining side down, press the seam allowances open.

5 Turn the valance right side out and press. Stitch the opening closed.

6 Center the valance over the mounting board, aligning the upper edge of the valance to the back of the board. Staple the valance to the mounting board, inserting the staples near the back of the board. Begin in the center and work toward the ends, spacing the staples 4" to 6" (10 to 15 cm) apart.

7 Mount the valance on the angle irons, replacing the screws in their original holes. Adjust the front corners of the valance to fall in gently rounded folds.

Butterfly and Stagecoach Valances

THESE VALANCES are made of folds of fabric held up with tabs or straps. They look as if they could be lowered, but they are stationary treatments. A butterfly valance has fanfolded fabric that droops in the center and flares at the sides. A stagecoach valance is rolled up from the bottom around a wooden dowel or PVC pipe and tied in place with straps.

Softly elegant (opposite)
In these gray-green butterfly valances, wide contrasting tabs hold the fanfolded fabric in place, allowing the lower edges to swag gently.

Setting the stage (top right)
This butterfly valance spans a deep-set window over a buffet. The mounting board for the valance projects out from the window frame far enough so that it doesn't interfere when the shade behind it is raised and lowered.

Inside-mount stagecoach (bottom right)
Contrasting lining draws attention to the rolled bottom of this inside-mounted stagecoach valance. Straps tied under the roll are cut from a striped fabric that coordinates with the floral print.

What you need to know

Butterfly and stagecoach valances can be **designed** slightly longer than most valances because of the visual weight at the lower edge. They are usually mounted outside the window frame but can be mounted inside if the casing is deep enough. For the instructions that follow, the butterfly valance is styled with *returns*. The stagecoach valance has no returns and is suitable for an inside mount or as a shallow outside-mounted valance. The straps for the butterfly valance are one continuous length. The stagecoach valance straps are two pieces that tie under the rolled fabric.

Medium-weight decorator **fabric** is suitable for either style of valance. Contrasting fabrics and companion prints are perfect for *lining* the stagecoach and for the straps on either style. *Underlining* gives the valance more body and prevents show-through when patterned fabrics are used.

Mount a stagecoach valance on a 1 × 2 board, whether it will be installed inside or outside the frame. Mount a butterfly valance on a mounting board that will project out from the window frame far enough to clear any existing treatment by 2" to 3" (5 to 7.5 cm). The length of the mounting board should be 2" (5 cm) wider than the window frame or 4" (10 cm) wider than any existing blinds or curtains.

Materials

- Mounting board
- Tools and hardware for installation
- Decorator fabrics for valance and straps
- Plain lining for butterfly valance; decorative lining for stagecoach valance
- Heavy-duty stapler
- 1³/₈" (3.5 cm) wooden dowel or PVC pipe, cut to finished width of valance
- Masking tape

Cutting directions

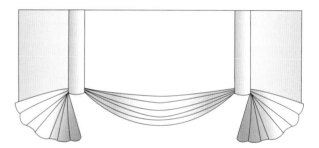

Butterfly valance

- The *cut length* of the fabric and lining is equal to the finished length (at the straps) plus 25" (63.5 cm).

- The *cut width* of the fabric and lining is equal to the finished width plus twice the *projection* of the mounting board plus 1" (2.5 cm). Piece full and partial fabric widths together as needed to obtain the cut width.

- For two straps with a finished width of 1¹/₂" (3.8 cm), cut two pieces 4" (10 cm) wide and twice the finished length plus 4" (10 cm).

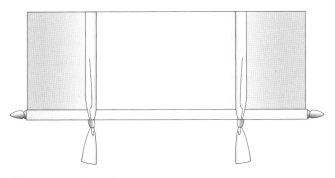

Stagecoach valance

- The cut length of the fabric and lining is equal to the finished length plus 14" (35.5 cm).

- The cut width of the fabric and lining is equal to the finished width plus 1" (2.5 cm). Piece full and partial fabric widths together as needed to obtain the cut width.

- For each strap, cut two fabric strips the full width of the fabric, with the cut width equal to the finished strap width plus 1/2" (1.3 cm).

Making a butterfly valance

1 Cut the board and cover it with fabric (page 123). Secure angle irons to the bottom of the mounting board, near the ends and at 45" (115 cm) intervals, using pan-head screws. Mount the board (page 124), centered above the window frame. Remove the screws that hold the mounting board to the angle irons, leaving the angle irons on the wall.

2 Seam fabric widths together, if necessary. Pin the outer fabric and lining right sides together. Stitch a 1/2" (1.3 cm) seam around the sides and lower edge; leave the upper edge unstitched.

3 Trim the lower corners diagonally. Press the lining seam allowance toward the lining. Turn the valance right side out, and press.

(continued)

3

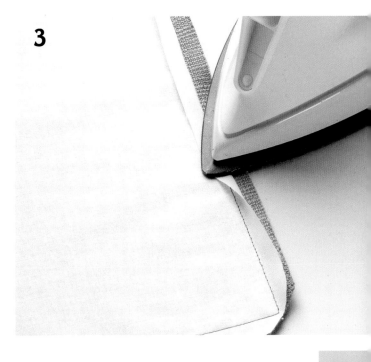

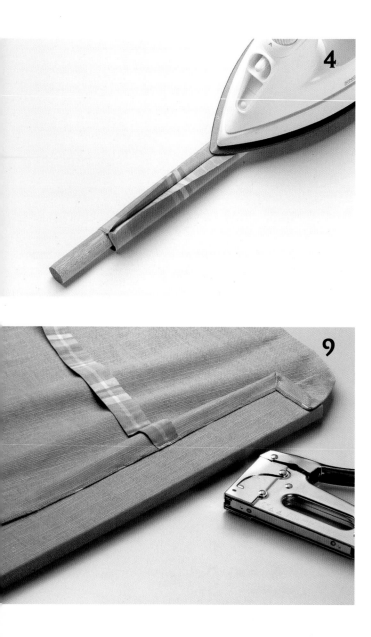

4 Fold one strap piece in half lengthwise, right sides together. Stitch a ½" (1.3 cm) seam along the long edge. Press the seam allowances open with the tip of the iron, taking care not to crease the fabric folds. Turn the strap right side out, centering the seam on the back; press. Repeat for the second strap.

5 Mark the location for the straps, 6" to 10" (15 to 25.5 cm) from each end, depending on the width of the valance. Pin one end of a strap, right side up, to the top of the valance at each mark.

6 Wrap the straps under the bottom of the valance. Pin the loose end of each strap in place on the lining side of the valance, raw edges even.

7 Stitch the outer fabric and lining together along the upper edge of the valance, catching the straps in the stitching. *Finish* the raw edges together, using zigzag stitches or by serging.

8 Mark lines on top of the mounting board 1" (2.5 cm) from the front and sides. Center the valance on the board, with the upper edge of the valance along the marked line. Staple the valance in place at 2" (5 cm) intervals. Apply two staples at each strap.

9 Wrap the sides of the valance around the ends of the mounting board, with the upper edges along the marked lines. Miter the corners. Staple the sides in place.

10 Mount the valance by reattaching the board to the angle irons.

11 Fanfold the lower 24" (61 cm) of the valance into five or six pleats, with the bottom fold turned under. Slip the straps under the folds.

12 Pull the folds down into a gentle swag. Adjust the folds near the straps.

58

Making a stagecoach valance

1 Follow steps 1 to 3 for the butterfly valance. Stitch the outer fabric and lining together along the upper edge of the valance. Finish the raw edges together, using zigzag stitches or by serging.

2 Fold a strap in half lengthwise, right sides together. Stitch the long edge and one short end, using ¼" (6 mm) seam allowances. Trim the corners diagonally. Turn the strap right side out and press, with the long seam on an outer edge. Repeat for all the straps, preparing two straps for each location.

3 Mark the locations for the straps at the top of the valance. Staple the valance to the mounting board, lapping the upper edge of the valance 1½" (3.8 cm) onto the top of the board. Do not place staples at the markings for the straps.

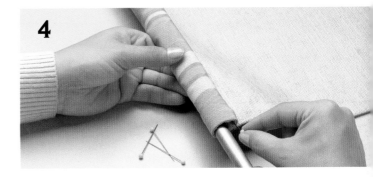

4 Center the dowel or PVC pipe on the right side of the valance at the lower edge; tape it in place. Roll up the valance to the desired finished length, and pin it to keep it from unrolling.

5 Sandwich the valance between two straps at each placement mark. Tie the ends under the rolled pole and adjust the length of the straps from the upper edge. Staple the straps to the board. Trim off any excess length at the top.

6 Mount the valance by reattaching the board to the angle irons. Hand-tack the rolled fabric to the front straps, catching only the back layer of fabric on the straps. Remove the pins that were preventing the fabric from unrolling.

Rod-Pocket Valances

Ｏ NE OF THE PRETTIEST toppers is the rod-pocket valance, with fabric gathered along a rod. With a wide *heading* and lots of *fullness*, a rod-pocket valance creates a feminine look just right for a little girl's room or powder room. The trend, though, is toward a short or no heading and less fullness. With this approach, the treatment will work in many rooms and décor styles.

No heading (opposite)
With a wide pocket and no heading, this rod-pocket valance looks less feminine.

Satin-stitched hem (top)
Green scalloped satin stitching edges the bottom of this sweet rod-pocket valance.

Turning corners (left)
The rod has been bent to follow the angle of this bathing alcove. The treatment softens the stark look of the privacy shades, and decorative beaded edging adds interest.

What you need to know

The rod pocket is the portion of the valance where the rod or pole is inserted; stitching lines at the top and bottom of the rod pocket keep the rod in place. To find the depth of the rod pocket, measure around the widest part of the rod; add ½" (1.3 cm) to this measurement, and divide by 2. The heading of a rod-pocket valance is the optional extension at the top that forms a ruffle when the valance is on the rod. The depth of the heading is the distance from the top of the finished valance to the top stitching line of the rod pocket.

Rod-pocket **designs** vary depending on the rod or pole used, whether or not there is a heading and how deep it is, and the *fullness* of the style. In the directions that follow, the valance is *lined* to add body and prevent light from showing through. For a lightweight, airy feeling, however, the lining can be left out.

Sheer, semisheer, lightweight, and medium-weight **fabrics** can be used. Generally, the lighter the fabric, the more fullness the valance can have, from triple fullness for sheer fabrics to one-and-one-half times fullness for a casual look with medium-weight fabric.

Several types of rods can be used for **mounting** rod-pocket valances, including flat rods in widths of 1", 2½", and 4½" (2.5, 6.5, and 11.5 cm). Wood and metal pole sets with elbows or finials can also be used and are available in several diameters. On a pole with elbows, the sides of the valance return to the wall. When a pole with finials is used, *returns* can be created at the sides of the valance by stitching an opening in the front of the rod pocket for inserting the pole.

Cutting directions

- The *cut length* of each valance piece is equal to the finished length (from the underside of the rod to the hem) plus twice the rod-pocket depth plus twice the heading height plus 4½" (11.5 cm).

- The *cut width* of the valance is equal to the rod length plus twice the *projection* of the rod, multiplied by the amount of fullness desired, usually two to two-and-one-half times. After calculating the full cut width, divide this number by the fabric width and round to the nearest number of full and half widths to piece together.

- The *lining* should be cut the same width as the decorator fabric but 3" (7.5 cm) shorter.

Making a rod-pocket valance

1 Seam fabric widths together, if necessary, adding any half widths at the sides. If an even number of full widths are needed, divide one in half lengthwise and add a half width to each side of the center full width to avoid a seam in the center of the valance.

| | heading |
| rod pocket |
| side seam | seam | | seam | side seam |
| | bottom hem |

2 Press under the lower edge 4" (10 cm) for the hem. Then unfold the pressed edge and turn the cut edge back, aligning it to the pressed fold line. Press the outer fold. Refold the lower edge, forming a 2" (5 cm) double-fold hem. Stitch, using a blindstitch or straight stitch.

3 Follow steps 1 and 2 for the lining, pressing under and stitching a 1" (2.5 cm) double-fold hem in the lining.

4 Pin the valance panel and lining panel wrong sides together, matching the raw edges at the sides and upper edge. Trim any excess at the sides so the panels are the same width. At the bottom, the lining panel will be 1" (2.5 cm) shorter than the valance panel. Press and stitch 1" (2.5 cm) double-fold side hems, handling the decorator fabric and lining as one fabric.

(continued)

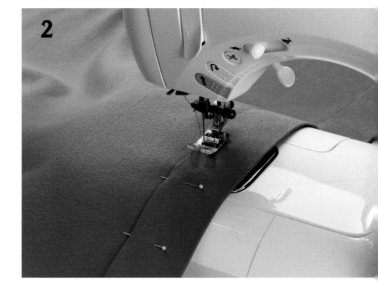

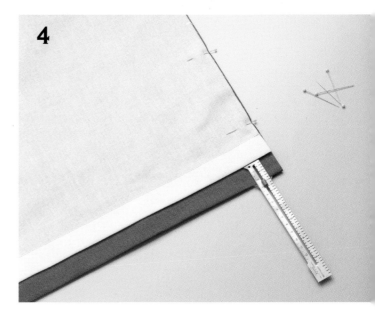

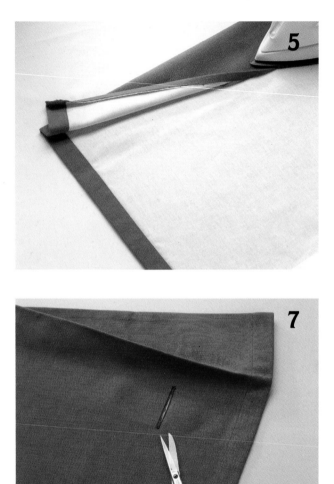

5 Press under ½" (1.3 cm) on the upper edge. Then press under an amount equal to the rod-pocket depth plus the heading depth. If the valance will be mounted on a pole with elbow returns, omit steps 6 and 7.

6 Measure the distance from the wall to the center of the pole. Unfold the upper edge of the valance. On the right side of the fabric, measure from the side of the valance a distance equal to this measurement; mark at the center of the rod pocket.

7 On the right side of the panel, stitch a buttonhole at the mark, from the top to the bottom of the rod pocket. Refold the upper edge of the panel along the pressed lines; pin.

8 Stitch close to the first fold; stitch again at the depth of the heading, using tape on the bed of the sewing machine as a stitching guide.

Installing a rod-pocket valance

Pole with wooden brackets and finials.
Remove the finials; insert the pole into the rod pocket with the ends of the pole extending through the buttonholes. Reattach the finials; mount the pole. Secure the return to the wooden bracket, using self-adhesive hook-and-loop tape.

Pole with keyhole bracket and finials.
Remove the finials; insert the pole into the rod pocket with the ends of the pole extending through the buttonholes. Reattach the finials. Insert the attachment screw through the fabric and into the back of the pole. Mount the pole by securing the screw in the keyhole. Attach a pin-on ring to the inner edge of the return, and secure it to a cup hook or tenter hook in the wall.

Pole with elbows.
Insert the pole through the rod pocket; pull the curtain back to expose the small attachment screws. Mount the pole on the brackets. Slide the curtain over the brackets.

Shaped Rod-Pocket Valances

A SOFT, CASUAL TREATMENT, the shaped rod-pocket valance forms a graceful arch. The curved hemline tapers into side tails. This version of a rod-pocket valance is *lined-to-the-edge* with a contrasting decorator fabric, which peeks out subtly along the lower edge. Shaped rod-pocket valances are often used over blinds or pleated shades to hide the top mechanism and soften the look. They are impressive when layered over floor-length draperies.

Lush and fringed (opposite)
Deep bullion fringe accents shaped hems in this formal sitting area. Without headings, the valances are more formal, yet their gathers soften the hardness of the louvered shutters.

Soft and feminine (left)
This shaped valance creates the perfect setting for a daybed. The modest heading adds frill without being excessive.

$\mathcal{W}$hat you need to know

The **design** most often seen is a single arch, with a center drop of one-third the window length and sides that extend down two-thirds the window length. For a narrower window, keep the arch relatively small to enhance and yet downplay the size. There can also be multiple small arches across a wider window. The tails can extend to the bottom of the window or even to the floor. The contemporary approach is a *fullness* of 1½ to 2 times the width of the window with short or no *headings*. The higher the heading, the more frilly and feminine the treatment will appear.

Lightweight and medium-weight decorator **fabrics** work best for both the face fabric and the *lining*.

Mount the valance on a 1" or 2½" (2.5 or 6.5 cm) utility curtain rod, as the fabric will completely cover the rod. You can also use a wooden pole.

Materials

- Decorator fabric for outer valance
- Chalk or removable marking pen
- Decorator fabric for lining
- Curtain rod or wooden pole
- Tools and hardware for installation

Cutting directions

- The *cut length* of each valance and lining piece is equal to the finished length at the longest point (from the underside of the rod to the hem) plus twice the rod-pocket depth plus twice the heading height plus 1" (2.5 cm).

- The *cut width* of the valance and lining is equal to the rod length plus twice the *projection* of the rod, multiplied by the amount of fullness desired, usually two to two-and-one-half times. After calculating the full cut width, divide this number by the fabric width and round to the nearest number of full and half widths to piece together.

- The cut length for the short center section of the valance is equal to the finished length at the shortest point plus twice the rod-pocket depth plus twice the heading height plus 1" (2.5 cm). This measurement is needed in step 1, opposite.

Making a shaped rod-pocket valance

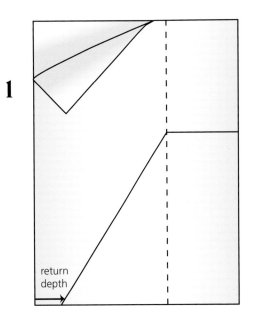

1

1 Seam the fabric widths as necessary. Divide the valance panel into thirds and mark. Fold the valance in half lengthwise; mark the cut length for the center portion from the fold to the one-third marking. Measure and mark the depth of the *return* at the side. Draw a straight line from the return mark to the one-third marking at the center length.

2 Round the upper corner at the one-third marking and the lower corner at the return, using a dinner plate or saucer as a guide. Pin the fabric layers together. Cut along the marked lines. Cut the lining panel, using the valance panel as a pattern.

3 Place the valance and lining panels right sides together. Stitch around the sides and lower edge in a ½" (1.3 cm) seam, leaving the upper edge open.

4 Press the lining seam allowances toward the lining. Clip the seam allowances at the curves, and trim the corners at the returns diagonally.

5 Turn the valance right side out; press the seamed edges. Press the upper edge under ½" (1.3 cm), folding both layers as one. Then press under an amount equal to the rod-pocket depth plus the heading depth. Stitch close to the first fold. Stitch again at the depth of the heading, using tape on the bed of the machine as a stitching guide.

6 Insert the curtain rod through the rod pocket; install the rod on the brackets. Distribute the fullness evenly along the rod.

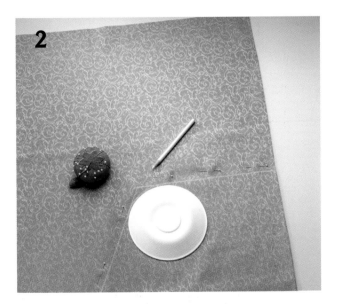

2

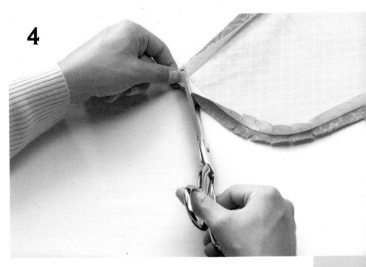

4

Gathered Pickup Valances

A GATHERED PICKUP valance looks quite complicated but is actually fairly easy to sew. It begins as a flat, lined rectangle with a rod pocket and *heading*. At evenly spaced intervals, vertical rows of tucks are sewn into the valance, drawing the lower section of the valance up into graceful bells. The fabric between the bells falls into gentle swags. Welting at the lower edge accents and supports the curves of the bells and swags. A contrasting fabric, used to line the valance, peeks from the inside of each bell.

Kingston (opposite)
A gathered pickup gives much the same look as this more complicated Kingston valance, which has graceful swags tucked up under box pleats. A Kingston valance requires a commercial pattern.

Rod-pocket pickup (top right)
A flat rectangle of fabric takes on a totally different look when gathered onto a rod and drawn up in bells. Fabric-covered welting emphasizes the undulating lower edge.

Board-mounted pickup (bottom right)
Matching valances above the sink and over the patio door tie the two areas of the room together.

What you need to know

When planning the **design** of the valance, work with enough full and half widths of fabric to equal about two-and-one-half times *fullness*. Bells are positioned at each seam and at each midpoint between seams. Though you usually shouldn't position prominent details of a window treatment at seams, this pattern of placement coincides with the placement of large motifs in most decorator fabrics, allowing the main motifs to fall in the center of each swag.

The valance hangs straight down at the *returns* to a length that is about 6" (15 cm) longer than the center of each swag. The shortest point at the back of each bell is about 2" (5 cm) shorter than the swags.

Medium-weight decorator **fabrics** work well for this valance. To add body and a slightly padded appearance, *interline* the valance with flannel. Select contrasting fabric for the *lining* and for the fabric-covered welting.

Mount the valance on a plain narrow pole with elbows or a utility rod just above and to the outside of the window frame.

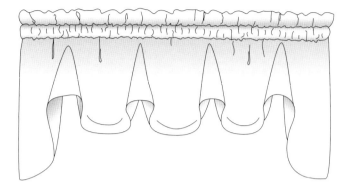

Materials

- Decorator fabric for valance
- Decorator fabric for contrasting lining
- Fabric-covered welting, twisted welting, or 1/2" (1.3 cm) filler cord and fabric for making fabric-covered welting
- Flannel interlining, optional
- Curtain rod
- Tools and hardware for installation

Cutting directions

- The *cut length* of the valance fabric is equal to the finished length at the side (from the underside of the rod to the hem) plus twice the rod-pocket depth plus twice the *heading* height plus 1" (2.5 cm).

- The *cut width* of the valance is equal to the rod length plus twice the *projection* of the rod, multiplied by two-and-one-half times fullness. After calculating the full cut width, divide this number by the fabric width and round to the nearest number of full and half widths to piece together.

- Cut the fabric for the contrast lining to the same length and width as the valance fabric.

- If interlining is desired, the cut width of the interlining fabric is equal to the total width of the valance fabric after seaming. The cut length of the interlining fabric is equal to the finished length of the valance. If possible, *railroad* the interlining to avoid seams.

- Cut *bias* fabric strips if making fabric-covered welting, following step 1 on page 125.

- In fabrics with large motifs, one complete vertical repeat will have two rows of motifs with staggered placement. One row will have two full motifs, while the second row will have one full motif in the center and two halves of another motif matching at the selvages. Cut the valance pieces with the primary motifs in the lower 12" to 15" (30.5 to 38 cm), so they will be more visible in the finished valance.

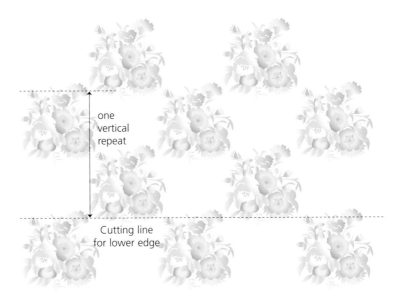

one vertical repeat

Cutting line for lower edge

Making a gathered pickup valance

1 Seam the valance fabric widths together. Repeat for the lining. Check to see that the valance and lining are exactly the same size.

2 Make fabric-covered welting (page 125), if desired, and stitch it to the lower edge of the valance; begin and end the welting ½" (1.3 cm) from the side edges. Alternatively, attach purchased welting. For a valance without interlining, omit step 3.

3 Seam the interlining, if necessary. Pin the interlining to the wrong side of the lining at the sides, with the lower edge of the interlining ½" (1.3 cm) above the lower edge of the lining. Baste within the ½" (1.3 cm) seam allowances on the sides.

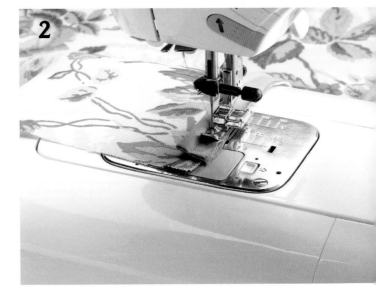

(continued)

5

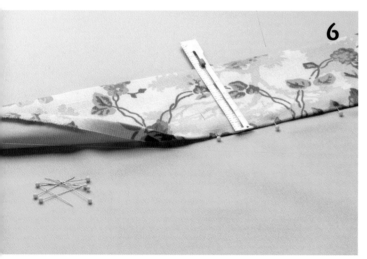

6

7

4 Place the valance and lining right sides together, matching the raw edges; pin along the sides and lower edge. Stitch ½" (1.3 cm) seams on the sides and lower edge, using a zipper foot and stitching with the valance fabric on top. Along the lower edge, stitch inside the previous stitching line, crowding the stitches against the welting.

5 Trim the lower corners diagonally. Turn the valance right side out. Press the sides and the lower edges. If the valance is interlined, smooth the interlining in place, checking to see that the upper edge of the interlining stops a distance from the upper edge of the valance equal to the heading depth plus the rod-pocket depth plus ½" (1.3 cm).

6 Press under ½" (1.3 cm) on the upper edge, turning under the valance and lining together. Then press under an amount equal to the heading depth plus the rod-pocket depth; pin.

7 Stitch close to the first fold; stitch again at the depth of the heading, using tape on the bed of the sewing machine as a stitching guide.

8 Lay the valance facedown on a flat surface. Mark for vertical rows of tucks at each seam and at each midpoint between the seams. The distance from the outer row of marks to the side edge equals the distance between rows. Measure up 10" (25.5 cm) from the lower edge for the placement of the first mark in each row. Place the remaining marks evenly spaced between the lower mark and the lower stitching line of the rod pocket, dividing the distance into three equal parts.

9 Thread a large-eyed needle with heavy thread. Insert the needle into the valance at the lowest mark in a row. Bring the needle back through to the lining side of the valance at the next mark and insert it back through ¼" (6 mm) above it. Repeat, taking a small stitch at each mark and running the thread on the right side of the valance. Bring the needle through at the lower stitching line of the rod pocket. Insert the needle back through ¼" (6 mm) to the side of the top stitch.

10 Make a second row of stitches alongside the first row back to the lowest mark. Cut the thread, leaving tails.

11 Repeat steps 9 and 10 for each marked row. Pull up the stitches to make three tucks in each row. Knot the thread securely.

12 Insert the rod into the rod pocket. Mount the rod; distribute the gathers evenly. Shape the bells and swags.

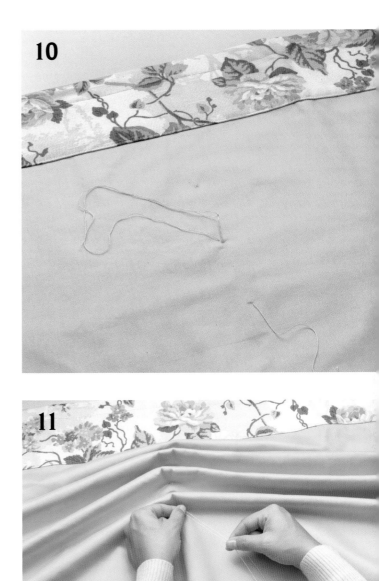

Tab Valances

Tab VALANCES are a classic, casual style, easy to create and hang. Choose short tabs—or even ties—for a cute, perky look; sew longer tabs or even knotted tabs for a more elegant appearance. Another popular option is the tab that flips over the rod and buttons at the front of the valance.

Tab valances are usually hung from a decorative rod. They can also be looped over decorative knobs or hooks. While the tabs must be equally spaced across the top, the distance apart as well as the length and style of the tabs will make your treatment unique.

Casual plaid (opposite)
A plaid, box-pleated, tab valance, edged at the top and bottom with narrow banding, is trendy and casual—perfect for this game room. Short, closely spaced tabs look just right over slender metal rods.

Shaped and fringed (top right)
A shaped lower edge enhanced with brush fringe makes an otherwise casual tab valance appear more elegant. Inverted box pleats at the corners help the returns hang without pulling.

Buttoned tabs (bottom right)
Neutral striped fabric is used for this stylish valance; the straps, sewn from the darker tone, are secured at the base with fabric-covered buttons in the lighter tone. Understated and timeless, this treatment makes the most of an unusual decorative rod.

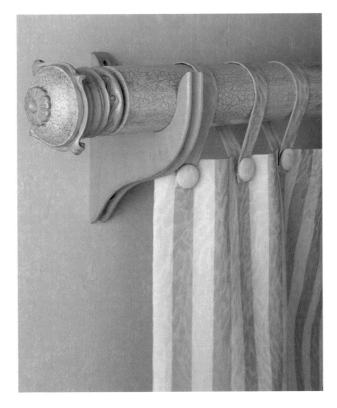

What you need to know

When you **design** your tab valance, experiment with different styles and sizes of tabs and the spacing between them. They should be evenly spaced at least 6" (15 cm) apart. The directions given are for tabs that loop over the rod with both ends sewn into the top seam. Tab valances range in length from 12" to 18" (30.5 to 46 cm), depending on the height of the window or existing curtains or shades.

Firmly woven, medium-weight decorator **fabrics** work well for tab valances because they have enough body to hold a straight line across the top between tabs. If you prefer a relaxed, slouchy look, choose lightweight pliable fabric for the valance. In the directions that follow, the valance is *self-lined*, omitting the need for a bottom hem. Deep seam allowances at the top and sides help support the edges. *Interlining* the valance with drapery *lining* gives it more body and prevents light show-through. The tabs can be of the same or contrasting material; even ribbons or decorative cording can be used.

Mount tab valances on decorative rods. Ideally, the top of the valance should cover the top of the window frame or *undertreatment*, so the rod is mounted higher, to allow for the length of the tabs. Test the tab style and length on the rod to determine the best height for mounting the rod.

Materials

- Decorator fabric for valance
- Matching or contrasting fabric for tabs
- Lining fabric for interlining
- Pole set or decorative curtain rod
- Tenter hooks or cup hooks for securing returns, optional
- Tools and hardware for installation

Cutting directions

- The *cut length* of the valance fabric is equal to twice the finished length plus 2" (5 cm).

- The *cut width* of the valance fabric is equal to two to two-and-one-half times the length of the pole or rod. Piece full and half widths of fabric together to obtain the needed width.

- The cut length of the interlining is equal to the finished length of the valance plus ½" (1.3 cm).

- The cut width of the interlining is equal to the cut width of the valance fabric.

- Cut a strip of fabric for each tab ½" (1.3 cm) wider and 2" (5 cm) longer than the finished size.

Making a tab valance

1 Fold a tab strip in half lengthwise, right sides together. Stitch a ¼" (6 mm) seam on the long edge. Repeat for the other tabs. Turn the tabs right side out; press. Edgestitch along both long edges.

2 Seam the valance fabric widths together as necessary; trim away selvages to prevent puckering. *Finish* the seam allowances together by serging or zigzagging. Press the seam allowances toward the sides of the valance.

3 Repeat step 2 for the interlining. Place the interlining over the wrong side of the valance, aligning the sides and upper edge. Baste within the ½" (1.3 cm) seam allowance.

4 Fold the tabs in half and pin them to the interlining side of the valance at the upper edge, raw edges matching. Place the end tabs 1" (2.5 cm) from each side; space the other tabs evenly between them. Machine-baste the tabs in place.

5 Fold the valance right sides together, aligning the long edges. Stitch 1" (2.5 cm) seams at the ends, being careful not to catch the tabs in the stitches. Stitch a 1" (2.5 cm) seam along the upper edge, encasing the tabs. Leave an opening in the upper edge for turning the valance right side out.

6 Trim the upper corners diagonally to within ⅛" (3 mm) of the stitching. With the interlining side down, press the seam allowances open.

7 Turn the valance right side out and press. Edgestitch along the top of the valance, closing the opening as you stitch. Stitch again 1" (2.5 cm) from the edge.

8 Hang the valance on the rod, spacing the tabs evenly. Adjust the *fullness* of the valance by rolling the fabric back at the tabs and forward between tabs. To create *returns*, hang the end tabs from tenter hooks or cup hooks on the wall and place the second tabs at the ends of the rod.

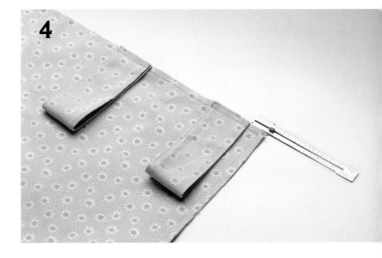

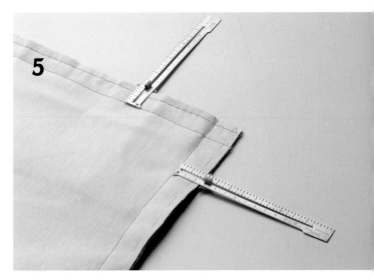

Pleated Valances

PLEATED VALANCES can be either crisply pressed and tailored or softly folded and elegant. Their symmetrical, geometrical look works well in many décors. These valances are easy to sew, too. They are just extra-wide *self-lined* rectangles with the excess width pleated out, stapled to mounting boards. Sketching the valance and making a pattern before sewing will ensure pleasing results.

Power of one (opposite)
A single inverted box pleat at the middle of a deep, banded valance makes a strong statement in this formal area. While centering the attention on the window, the valance also hides the hardware for the draperies and Roman shade.

Knife pleats (top)
Knife pleats play off of the plaid pattern.

Timeless toile (left)
Inverted box pleats in a lovely toile pattern grace not only the window, but also the canopy and dust ruffle. The crisp tailoring prevents so much fabric from overwhelming the small room.

What you need to know

Knife pleats and box pleats are the two basic **design** styles used for a pleated valance. Knife pleats are a series of sharp creases of equal size and spacing, usually 1" to 2" (2.5 to 5 cm), all turned in the same direction. For symmetry, knife-pleated valances are often divided in the center, with pleats turned toward the outer edges. Pleats can be arranged continuously from the center outward or in clusters of three or more pleats separated by spaces.

A box pleat looks like two knife pleats turned away from each other. Box pleats are generally deeper than knife pleats and are separated by wider spaces. This style is especially appealing when the folds are left unpressed for a softer look.

For inverted box pleats, the excess fabric of the pleat is folded to the inside. A valance can have continuous inverted box pleats of equal size and spacing, ending with one at each front corner. Fewer box pleats can be placed farther apart, perhaps accenting structural divisions of the window. For instance, you often see simple valances that have an inverted box pleat at each corner and one at the center.

It is necessary to make a paper pattern of the valance, following steps 1 to 3, opposite. The pattern will help determine pleat size, spacing, and placement of seams, allowing for adjustments before the panel width is cut. Any seams must be hidden in the folds of the pleats. If possible, *railroad* the fabric to eliminate seams.

To prevent the excess bulk of a hem, pleated valances are *self-lined*. They can be *interlined* with lightweight drapery *lining*, if necessary, to prevent the pattern on the back from showing through to the front.

Choose **fabric** for pleated valances according to the number and style of the pleats. Heavy pleating will obviously distort the pattern of the fabric, so plain colors or smaller,

all-over prints are more desirable than large prints. Larger prints are suitable for valances with fewer pleats. Striped and plaid fabrics can work very well for pleated valances as long as the pleats coincide with the fabric pattern.

Pleated valances are **mounted** on boards installed above and outside the window frame. If there is no *undertreatment*, a 1 × 4 board works well. If the valance goes over an existing treatment, it must have a deeper *projection*.

front view

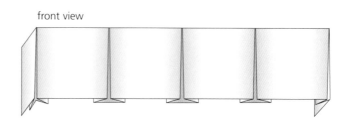

Materials

- Graph paper
- Roll of paper, such as adding machine paper
- Decorator fabric
- Drapery lining, for interlining valance, optional
- Decorative trim, for valance with unpressed pleats, optional
- Heavy paper, for pressing pleats
- Mounting board
- Heavy-duty stapler
- Tools and hardware for installation

Cutting directions

- The *cut length* of the valance fabric is twice the finished length plus 3" (7.5 cm).

- Cut full crosswise widths of fabric and piece them together so they are wider than the pattern. This will allow you to hide seams in pleats. Cut the fabric to the exact width in step 1, below.

- The cut length of the interlining is equal to the finished length plus 1½" (3.8 cm); the *cut width* is the same as the cut width of the valance fabric.

Making the pattern

1 Draw the valance to scale on graph paper, indicating the finished length, width, return depth, and placement of the pleats. *Returns* of 3½" (9 cm) or more can have two or more knife pleats or half of an inverted box pleat. Leave the valance flat on smaller returns. Plan the pleat depths, space sizes, and any seam placements; don't overlap pleats. For a striped or plaid valance, follow the fabric pattern to determine the pleat and space sizes. Check to see that the space measurements add up to the finished width.

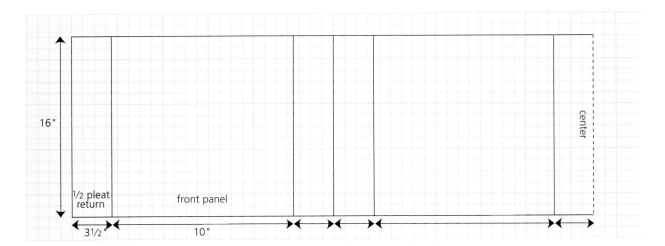

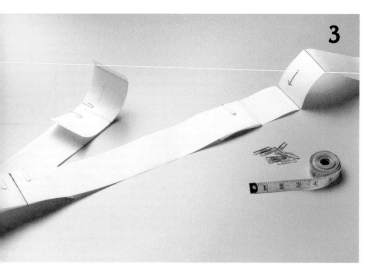

2 Unroll adding machine paper on a flat surface. Mark a 1/2" (1.3 cm) side seam allowance at the end. Measure and mark all spaces and pleats as determined in step 1. Mark the folds with solid lines; mark the placement lines with dotted lines. Indicate the direction of the folds with arrows. Mark the pattern for the entire width of the valance, ending with a 1/2" (1.3 cm) seam allowance at the opposite end; cut the paper.

3 Fold the pleats as marked. Measure the folded pattern to see that it equals the desired finished width, including the returns; adjust a few pleats, if necessary.

Making a pleated valance

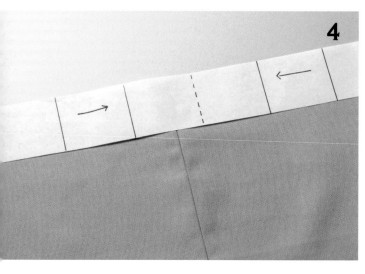

4 Seam the fabric widths as necessary. Trim the seam allowances to 1/4" (6 mm); press them open. Lay the valance pattern over the seamed fabric, aligning the seams to points in the pattern where they will be hidden in pleats; cut the fabric to the width of the pattern.

5 Pin the interlining, if desired, to the wrong side of the valance, matching the upper edges and ends. Fold the end of the valance in half lengthwise, right sides together. Sew a 1/2" (1.3 cm) seam on the outer edge of the return. Repeat for the opposite end of the valance.

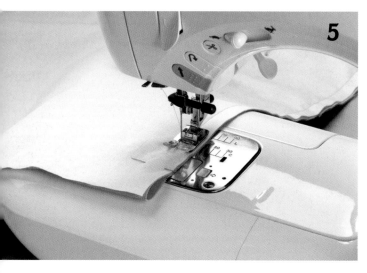

6 Turn the valance right side out; press. Match the upper raw edges. If your valance has interlining, it should extend to the lower fold of the valance. Machine-baste the layers together 1/2" (1.3 cm) from the upper raw edges. For a valance with unpressed pleats, apply trim to the lower edge, if desired.

7 Lay the valance faceup on a flat surface; lay the pattern over the upper edge of the valance, aligning the end seam lines to the seamed outer edges. Transfer the pattern markings to the valance. Repeat along the lower edge.

8 Pin the pleats in place along the upper and lower edges and center of the valance. Measure the valance width; adjust if necessary, distributing the adjusted amount among several pleats. If unpressed pleats are desired, omit step 9.

9 Press the pleats on the face of the valance, removing the pins from one pleat at a time; insert heavy paper under each pleat as it is pressed, to avoid imprinting. Replace the pins along the upper edge.

10 Stitch the pleats in place across the valance, 1½" (3.8 cm) from the upper edge; remove the pins. *Finish* the upper edge, by serging or zigzag stitching.

11 Cut the mounting board and cover it with fabric (page 123). Secure angle irons to the bottom of the mounting board, near the ends and at 45" (115 cm) intervals, using pan-head screws. Mount the board (page 124), centered above the window frame. Remove the screws that hold the mounting board to the angle irons, leaving the angle irons on the wall.

12 Position the valance on the mounting board, using the stitching line as a guide to extend the upper edge 1½" (3.8 cm) onto the top of the board; position the end pleats at the front corners of the board. Staple the valance in place at the returns. Clip the fabric at the corner pleats close to the stitching line to control the bulk. Staple the valance in place; ease or stretch the valance slightly to fit the board, if necessary. Mount the valance by re-attaching the board to the angle irons.

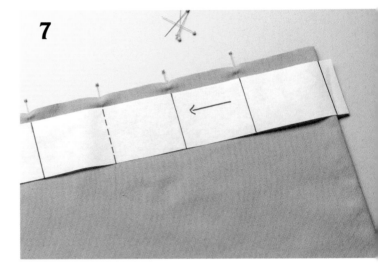

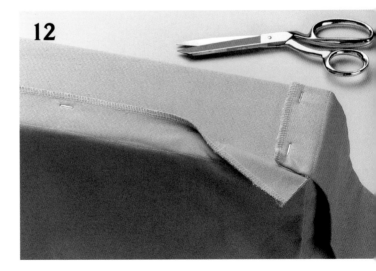

Pleated Valances with Shaped Hems

THESE VALANCES are often seen crowning a drapery, blinds, or shades. Less stiff than a cornice, the shaped hem valance frames the window with graceful curves and gentle lines.

For a stylish variation, the lower edge can be shaped into curves or angles.

Pleats and scallops (opposite)
Inverted-box-pleat valances with soothing scalloped hemlines top the sheer draperies in a girl's room. Pleats were planned to coincide with the horizontal pattern repeat of the blue floral fabric.

Sheffield valance (top right)
The hemline of the Sheffield valance swoops between kicky box pleats lined in a contrasting fabric. While often seen in formal settings, this Sheffield is very much at home in a country kitchen.

Softened squares (bottom right)
Dense brush fringe along the softly undulating hemlines softens the rigid square pattern of the fabric in these valances. Stacked box pleats near the sides add interesting dimension.

What you need to know

The **design** options for the lower edge are up to your imagination. Begin by sketching the valance to scale on graph paper. Determine the style and number of pleats. Shape the lower edge to complement the pleats and perhaps accent structural details of the window itself. For best results, avoid severe angles and sharp curves. Valance and *lining* pieces are cut using a full-size pattern.

Choose medium-weight decorator **fabric** in a plain color, small print, or a larger pattern that will work well with the design of your valance. Because the lining may be visible along the lower edge in some areas, line the valance with the same fabric or a coordinating fabric.

Pleated valances with shaped hems are **mounted** on boards installed above and outside the window frame. If there is no *undertreatment*, a 1 × 4 board works well. If the valance goes over an existing treatment, it must have a deeper *projection*.

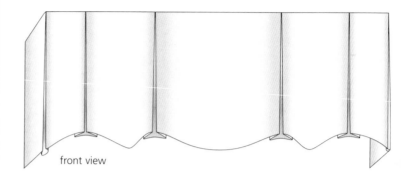

front view

Materials

- Graph paper
- Roll of wide paper, such as inexpensive tablecloth paper or tracing paper
- Designing tool, such as flexible curve or curved ruler
- Decorator fabric
- Lightweight decorator fabric in accent color or coordinating print, for lining
- Heavy paper, for pressing pleats
- Mounting board
- Tools and hardware for installation
- Heavy-duty stapler

Making the pattern

1 Draw the valance to scale on graph paper, indicating the finished length, width, *return* depth, and placement of the pleats. Returns of 3½" (9 cm) or more can have two or more knife pleats or half of an inverted box pleat. Leave the valance flat on smaller returns. Plan the pleat depths, space sizes, and any seam placements; don't overlap pleats. For a striped or plaid valance, follow the fabric pattern to determine the pleat and space sizes. Check to

see that the space measurements add up to the finished width. Draw the shape of the lower edge, using one of these options or your own design.

(continued)

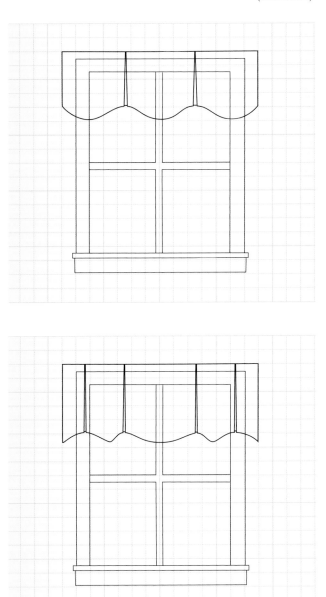

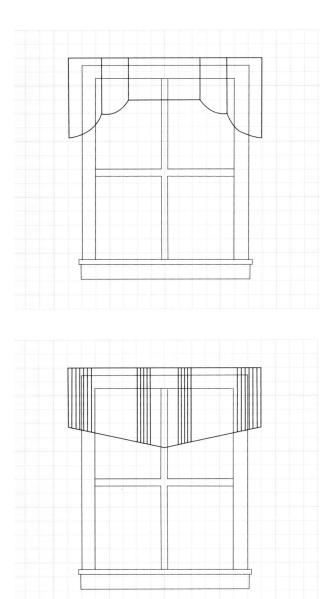

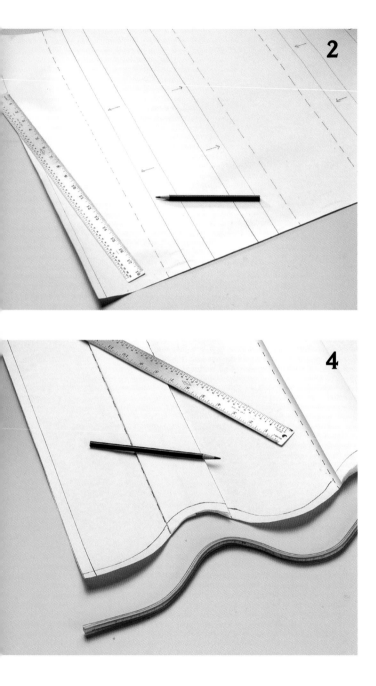

2   Unroll the wide paper; cut the paper with the length equal to the desired finished length of the valance at the long point plus 2" (5 cm). Mark a ½" (1.3 cm) side seam allowance at one end. Measure and mark all the spaces and pleats as determined in step 1. Mark the folds with solid lines; mark the placement lines with dotted lines. Indicate the direction of the folds with arrows. Mark the pattern for the entire width of the valance, ending with a ½" (1.3 cm) seam allowance at the opposite end; cut the paper.

3   Fold the pleats as marked. Measure the folded pattern to see that it equals the desired finished width, including the returns; adjust a few pleats, if necessary.

4   Draw the shaped seam line of the lower edge on the folded pattern, following your graphed sketch, with the longest point ½" (1.3 cm) above the cut edge of the paper. Draw curved lines, using a designing tool such as a flexible curve or curved ruler; draw angled lines, using a straightedge. Add a ½" (1.3 cm) seam allowance below the seam line. Cut out the pattern.

Cutting directions

- The *cut length* of the valance fabric is the finished length at the longest point plus 2" (5 cm).

- Cut full crosswise widths of fabric and piece them together so they are wider than the pattern. This will allow you to hide seams in pleats. Cut the fabric to the exact width in step 1, opposite.

- Cut the lining with the same length and width as the valance fabric.

Making a shaped pleated valance

1 Seam the fabric widths as necessary. Trim the seam allowances to ¼" (6 mm); press them open. Lay the valance pattern over the seamed fabric, aligning the seams to points in the pattern where they will be hidden in pleats; cut the fabric to the width of the pattern.

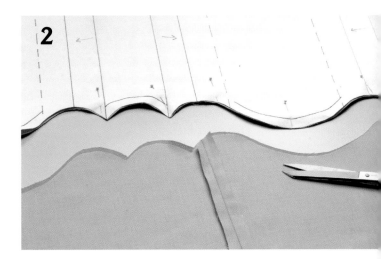

2 Place the valance fabric and lining right sides together; pin the pattern in place, aligning the upper edges and sides. Cut the valance fabric and lining along the lower edge of the pattern.

3 Remove the pattern. Pin the valance and lining together along the lower edge and sides; stitch a ½" (1.3 cm) seam.

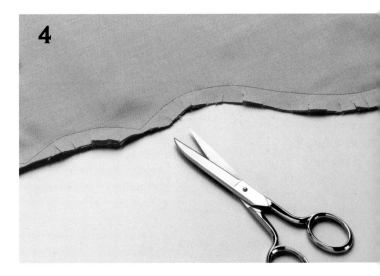

4 Trim the outer corners, clip into the inner corners, and clip the seam allowances on the curves. Complete the valance as on pages 84 and 85, steps 6 to 12.

Balloon Valances

HEN A ROOM needs a focal point, the romantic balloon valance may be just right. The balloon valance is a series of inverted box pleats that are raised into soft billows along the lower edge. Graceful folds of fabric dip deeply into the top third of the window. The treatment can be sewn from one fabric, like the examples shown here, or with insets of contrasting fabric in the folds of each pleat to create more interest.

Focal point (opposite)
Multiple poufs conform to the contours of a bay window and show off the blue-on-yellow floral print, giving the room a definite focal point.

Padded effect (right)
Tassel fringe underlines the gentle curve of this generous balloon valance. The subtle gold check fabric has a soft, plump look because it has cushiony interlining.

*W*hat you need to know

To help you **design** your balloon valance, draw a diagram that shows the finished width, length, and *projection* of the valance. Your valance can have only two pleats (one at each corner) or several pleats spaced evenly at least 12" (30.5 cm) apart. After determining the number of pleats, to determine the exact space between pleats, divide this number into the valance width. Including the pleats at the outer front corners, there will be one more pleat in the valance than the number of spaces.

Balloon valances require at least two times *fullness*. They can be made from one **fabric** panel that is folded into inverted box pleats or the pleat inserts can be a contrasting fabric, as in the directions that follow. Choose lightweight to medium-weight fabrics that have enough body to hold the poufed shape without being too stiff.

Balloon valances are board **mounted**, which keeps light from shining up through the top of the treatment. The mounting board should extend 2" (5 cm) beyond the window frame or *undertreatment* on each side and have a *return* depth 2" (5 cm) deeper than the undertreatment or at least 4" (10 cm) if there is no undertreatment. A narrow utility curtain rod with returns equal to the depth of the mounting board stabilizes the lower edge and holds it away from the window or undertreatment.

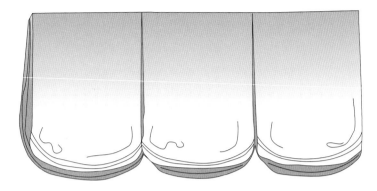

Materials

- Decorator fabric for main valance
- Contrasting decorator fabric for the pleat inserts
- Lining fabric
- Mounting board
- Plastic rings
- Shade cord
- Utility curtain rod with same projection as the mounting board
- Tools and hardware for installation
- Heavy-duty stapler

Cutting directions

- From the main valance fabric, cut a piece for each space section with the width equal to the finished width of the space plus 1" (2.5 cm). The *cut length* of each piece is equal to the finished length plus 14" (35.5 cm).

- Cut the fabric for each return section with the width equal to the projection of the mounting

94

board plus 1" (2.5 cm). The cut length of each piece is equal to the finished length plus 14" (35.5 cm).

- Cut the contrasting fabric for the pleat inserts 21" (53.5 cm) wide with length equal to the finished length plus 14" (35.5 cm). If the projection of the mounting board is less than 5" (12.7 cm), trim the corner pleat inserts to equal twice the projection of the mounting board plus 11" (28 cm).

- Cut a piece of *lining* fabric to match each of the space sections, return sections, and pleat insert sections.

- Cut a facing strip 2½" (6.5 cm) wide and 1" (2.5 cm) longer than the finished width of the valance (including returns).

Making a balloon valance

1 Pin a decorator fabric piece and matching lining piece wrong sides together. *Finish* the sides together by serging or zigzag stitching. Repeat for each piece of the valance.

2 Pin the pleat insert for the left end of the valance over the left return section, right sides together. Stitch a ½" (1.3 cm) seam.

3 Pin a space section to the other side of the pleat insert, right sides together. Stitch a ½" (1.3 cm) seam. Continue to join sections, alternating pleat inserts and spaces. End with the right pleat insert and the right return section. Press the seam allowances open.

(continued)

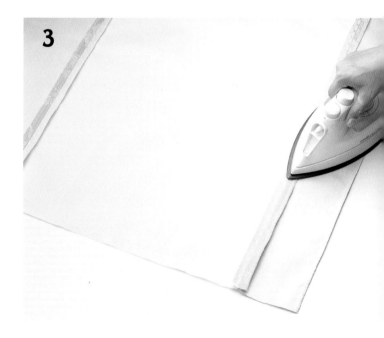

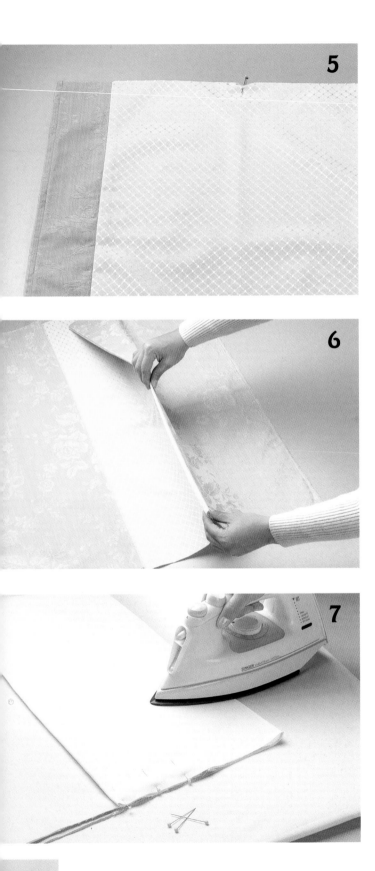

4 Turn under and press ½" (1.3 cm) side hems; stitch.

5 Mark the center of each pleat insert along the upper and lower edges. If the return is less than 5" (12.7 cm), measure from the inner seam of the return a distance equal to twice the return; mark.

6 Fold under the pleats at the seam lines; press. Bring the pressed seams together to the marks. Pin the pleats in place at the upper and lower edges. The side hems should be hidden under the end pleats.

7 Press the folded edges of all the pleat inserts, turning the valance back and pressing only on the pleat insert to avoid imprinting the edges to the right side of the valance.

8 Stitch the pleats in place across the valance, 1½" (3.8 cm) from the upper edge. Finish the upper edge by serging or zigzag stitching. Stitch ½" (1.3 cm) from the lower edge to secure the pleats.

9 Press under ½" (1.3 cm) on the short ends and one long side of the facing strip. Pin the other long side to the bottom of the valance, right sides together. Stitch a ½" (1.3 cm) seam. Turn the fac-ing to the wrong side of the valance; press. Edgestitch along the inner fold, forming a casing for the lower rod.

10 Mark positions for four rings in columns at the center of each pleat insert, placing the bottom marks at the top of the casing and spacing the others 3" (7.5 cm) apart.

11 Stitch a ring at each mark, stitching only through the lining and insert fabric in the pleats.

12 Thread a length of shade cord through the rings of the first column and tie the rings together. Repeat for each column.

13 Cut the mounting board and cover it with fabric (page 123). Mount the board (page 124), centered above the window frame. Remove the board, leaving the angle irons on the wall.

14 Place the valance on the mounting board, using the stitching line as a guide to extend the upper edge 1½" (3.8 cm) onto the top of the board. Place the end pleats at the front corners of the board. Staple the valance in place.

15 Mount the valance on the angle irons, replacing the screws in their original holes. Insert the utility rod into the bottom casing. Adjust the billows at the lower edge of the valance.

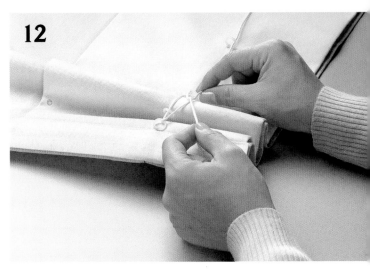

Cloud Valances

THE CLOUD VALANCE is feminine, romantic, and eye-catching. It is gathered across the top, either by making a rod pocket and mounting the valance on a curtain rod (as in the directions that follow) or by gathering the top with shirring tape and securing it to a mounting board. The lower edge is raised into a series of soft billows by sewing in columns of rings and tying them together.

Different depths (opposite)
An extra-wide rod pocket creates a grand top for this sheer cloud valance. Three graceful swags of different depths are created by tying the two inner columns of rings tighter than the outer columns.

Ruffles (top)
Long cloud valances over sidelights draw the eye to the glass ceiling in this solarium. Ruffles emphasize the dramatic curves and folds at the lower edge.

Single pouf (left)
This single-pouf cloud valance is made by sewing a rod pocket at the top and bottom. In a deep window casing, tension rods hold the valance in place, the lower one tucked up and under the fabric to puff out the extra fullness and length.

$\mathcal{W}$hat you need to know

When you **design** a cloud valance, the pouf sizes can all be the same or they can vary in width and length. Columns of rings should be placed at seams between fabric widths and 18" to 24" (46 to 61 cm) apart, so, depending on the fabric width, there will either be two or three poufs per fabric width.

Lightweight **fabrics,** including sheers and semisheers, and soft medium-weight fabrics work best for cloud valances. The amount of *fullness* can vary. If using a medium-weight decorator fabric, two to two-and-one-half times fullness works well. For lighter fabric, three times fullness can be used. *Lining* gives the cloud valance extra body to hold the shape of the poufs and keeps light from shadowing through.

Mount the valance using a utility curtain rod. If the cloud valance will be installed over a shade or blind, the valance should be wide enough and project out far enough so it doesn't interfere with the operation of the *undertreatment*. A second curtain rod mounted under the lower edge of the cloud valance keeps the valance at the necessary *projection*.

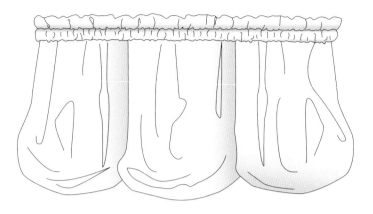

Materials

- Decorator fabric for cloud valance
- Lining fabric, optional
- Plastic rings
- Shade cord
- Two utility curtain rods of equal projections
- Tools and hardware for installation

Cutting directions

- The *cut length* of each valance piece is equal to the finished length (from the underside of the rod to the hem) plus twice the rod-pocket depth plus twice the *heading* height plus 18" (46 cm).

- The *cut width* of the valance is equal to the rod length plus twice the projection of the rod, multiplied by the amount of fullness desired, usually two to two-and-one-half times. After calculating the full cut width, divide this number by the fabric width and round to the nearest number of full and half widths to piece together.

- Cut the lining the same width and length as the decorator fabric.

Making a cloud valance

1 Seam fabric widths together, using only full and half widths and adding the half widths at the sides. If an even number of full widths are needed, divide one in half and add a half width to each side of the center full width to avoid a seam in the center of the valance. Repeat for the lining, if desired.

2 Pin the valance and lining wrong sides together, aligning all edges. Trim any excess so the panels are the same size. Turn under and stitch 1" (2.5 cm) double-fold side hems, handling the decorator fabric and lining as one fabric.

3 Press under ½" (1.3 cm) on the upper edge. Then press under an amount equal to the rod-pocket depth plus the heading depth. Stitch close to the first fold; stitch again at the depth of the heading, using tape on the bed of the sewing machine as a stitching guide.

4 Turn under and stitch a 1" (2.5 cm) double-fold hem at the bottom.

5 Lay the valance facedown on the work surface. Mark positions for rings in columns at the side hems and at each seam, placing the bottom marks at the top of the bottom hem. Space one or two additional columns of marks between seams. Place four marks in each column, spaced 6" (15 cm) apart.

6 Stitch a ring at each mark, stitching through the lining and valance fabric.

7 Thread a length of shade cord through the rings of the first column and tie the rings together. Leave long tails of cord. Repeat for each column.

8 Insert the curtain rod in the upper rod pocket and mount the valance. Adjust the fullness evenly.

9 Mount the lower rod under the valance, even with the clusters of tied rings. Tie the cording tails to the rod to keep the poufs in position and away from the undertreatment. Adjust the poufs.

Upholstered Cornices

AN UPHOLSTERED CORNICE is a formal, tailored top treatment made by covering a wooden frame with fabric. The frame, like a box with an open back and bottom, is first padded with foam or batting to round the corners for a soft, upholstered look. Fabric-covered welting or twisted cord welting can be used to define the upper and lower edges of the cornice.

Building a cornice from plywood or pine boards takes only very basic carpentry skills. Any imperfections will be covered with padding and fabric. The front of your cornice can be cut straight across or can be shaped with curves and angles.

A cornice not only frames and finishes a window treatment by hiding the hardware, but also provides good insulation and light control because it encloses the top of the treatment.

Arched form (opposite)
These dramatic arched cornices are a grand focal point for a formal dining area. Ornate metal medallions accent the upper corners.

Nail head (top right)
A simple rectangular box cornice has been distinctively detailed with hammered brass nail heads.

Understated (bottom right)
Subtle shaping at the bottom of these cornices softens their appearance. Mounted at ceiling height, they hide the drapery hardware and create the illusion that the windows are higher than they are.

What you need to know

Design your cornice to clear the curtain or drapery hardware by 2" to 3" (5 to 7.5 cm) and extend at least 2" (5 cm) beyond the end of the drapery or window frame on each side. These measurements are the cornice *inside* measurements. Allow for the thickness of the wood when cutting.

In the directions that follow, the upper and lower edges of the cornice are defined with welting. Disregard the references to welting if you prefer your cornice without it.

Medium-weight, firmly woven decorator **fabrics** and upholstery fabrics are suitable for cornices. *Railroad* the fabric on a cornice to eliminate seams on plain fabrics and fabrics with nondirectional prints. If the fabric cannot be railroaded, place the seams inconspicuously, never in the center. Prints should be centered or balanced on the cornice front.

To **mount** your cornice, use enough angle irons to support and distribute the weight. It is difficult or impossible to insert screws into the wall working up inside a narrow box, so it is important to follow step 16 (page 107) when you install your cornice.

Materials

- Decorator fabric
- Lining fabric
- Contrasting fabric for welting
- Plywood or pine boards, 1/2" (1.3 cm) thick, for the front, top, and sides of the cornice box
- Carpenter's glue
- Sixpenny finishing nails
- Polyester upholstery batting or polyurethane foam, 1/2" (1.3 cm) thick
- Filler cord, 5/32" (3.8 mm) thick for making welting
- Heavy-duty stapler
- Cardboard upholstery stripping, enough to cover top and bottom edges
- Spray foam adhesive
- Tools and hardware for installation

Cutting directions

- For the face piece, cut decorator fabric 6" (15 cm) wider than the front and sides, and 3" (7.5 cm) longer than the height of the cornice.

- Cut a 4" (10 cm) inner *lining* strip from decorator fabric the same width as the face piece.

- Cut a strip of lining fabric the same width as the face piece and 2" (5 cm) shorter than the cornice height.

- Cut decorator fabric for the dustcover (fabric that covers the top of the cornice box) 1" (2.5 cm) larger than the cornice top.

- Cut a strip of batting or foam to cover the front and sides of the cornice.

- Cut 1½" (3.8 cm) bias strips of contrasting fabric to make fabric-covered welting. You will need a length slightly longer than the edges to be welted.

Making an upholstered cornice

1 For the cornice box, measure and cut the cornice top. Cut the front the same width as the top and the desired finished height. Shape the lower edge of the front, if desired. Cut the sides the same height as the cornice front and the depth of the top piece plus the thickness of the wood.

2 Glue the top to the front board first. Nail to secure. Then attach the sides, first gluing in place and then securing with nails. Allow the glue to set.

3 Prepare the welting as in steps 1 to 4 on page 125. Stitch the welting to the lower edge of the face piece in a ½" (1.3 cm) seam, raw edges even.

4 Sew the lower (welted) edge to the inner lining strip, right sides together. Sew the free edge of the inner strip to the lining strip. Press the seam allowances toward the lining.

5 Mark the center of the face piece at the top and bottom. Mark the center of the cornice at the top and bottom. Place the wrong side of the face fabric on the outside of the cornice, with the lower (welted) seam on the lower front edge of the cornice; match the center markings. Staple in place at the center.

(continued)

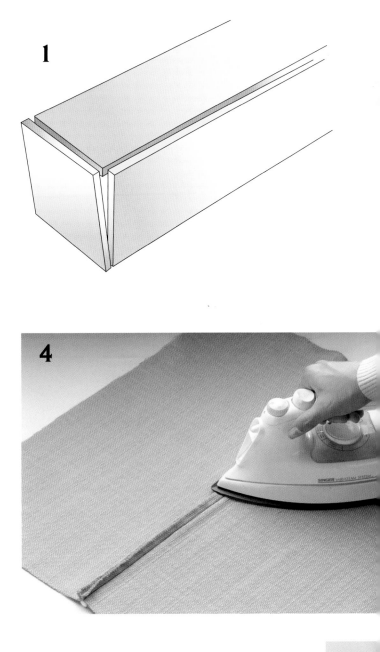

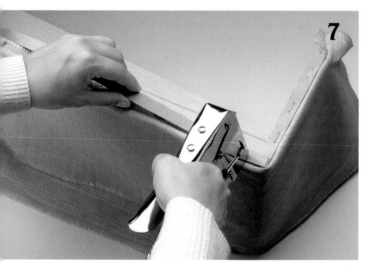

6 Pull the seam allowances taut to the corners of the cornice, and staple in place. Staple every 4" (10 cm) from the center to the ends, keeping the lower (welted) seam aligned to the front edge of the cornice.

7 Place cardboard stripping tight against the lower (welted) seam. Staple every 1" to 1½" (2.5 to 3.8 cm). Cut and overlap the stripping at the corners.

8 Fold the lining to the inside. Fold under the raw edge, and staple at the inside of the box where the top and face meet. At the lower corners, miter the fabric and staple close to the corner. Tuck excess fabric into the upper corners, and staple.

9 Open the welting seam back to the edge of the cornice. Trim the welting to 1" (2.5 cm). Trim out the cording even with cornice back edge to reduce bulk. Staple the lining to the back edge of the cornice; trim the excess lining. Staple the welting end to the back edge of the cornice.

10 Turn the cornice faceup. Apply spray adhesive to the front and sides. Place the padding over the glued surface, and smooth it taut over the front and sides. Allow the glue to set.

11 Fold the face fabric over the front of the cornice. Gently smooth the fabric toward the top of the cornice, keeping the padding tucked snug into the corners and along the lower edge.

12 Staple the face fabric to the cornice top at the center and ends, keeping the fabric taut but not stretched too tightly. Starting at the center, turn under the raw edge and staple it to the cornice top. Smoothing the fabric as you go, work first toward one end and then the other, placing staples 1½" (3.8 cm) apart.

13 Pull the fabric around the cornice end to the top back corner, removing any slack; staple. Fold the side fabric to the back edge; staple. Trim the excess fabric at the back edge.

14 Fold the fabric diagonally at the corners to form miters. Staple at the corners and across the ends.

15 Staple welting to the sides and front of the cornice top, with the welting stitching line along the front and side edges. On the cornice front, place the dustcover over the welting, with right sides together and raw edges even. Staple cardboard stripping at the front. Fold under the sides of the dustcover even with the sides of the cornice. Insert cardboard stripping into the folds. Pull the fabric to the top of the cornice, and staple in place close to the folds. Fold under the back edge of the dustcover and staple it in place.

16 Screw angle irons to the underside of the cornice top near the ends and at 36" (91.5 cm) intervals, using pan-head screws. Hold the cornice in its proper position above the window, and mark the screw holes for the angle irons on the wall. Lower the cornice. Remove the angle irons, and attach them to the wall. Mount the cornice by reattaching it to the angle irons on the wall.

Rod-Pocket Mock Cornices

OP TREATMENTS that resemble cornices can be made without carpentry or upholstery techniques. Mock cornices are mounted on flat curtain rods that are 4½" (11.5 cm) wide. Fusible fleece applied inside the rod pocket gives the treatment a padded look. The top and bottom of the rod pocket are accented with fabric-covered welting or twisted cord welting. For added flair and extra length, a pleated or gathered skirt is sewn below the rod pocket.

These versatile top treatments can be used to dress up windows that have existing treatments, such as vertical or horizontal blinds, pleated shades, or curtains. If you have sleeve valances on rods that are looking outdated, mock cornices will freshen the look without the expense of new rods.

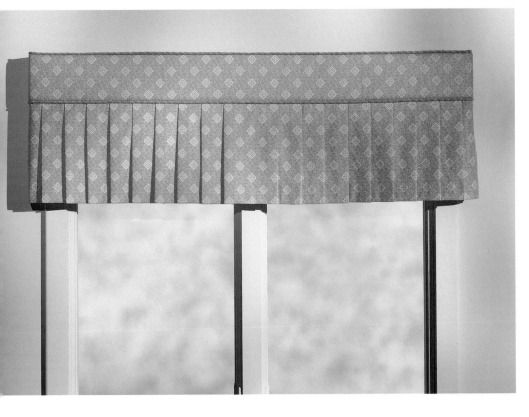

Gathered skirt (opposite)
The gathered skirt on this mock cornice has a soft, feminine appearance, providing a relaxed look while hiding the mechanisms of the shade.

Pleated skirt (left)
Knife pleating on the skirt of this mock cornice looks crisp and tailored. Narrow twisted cord welting accentuates the flat sleeve.

What you need to know

Design your mock cornice with either a pleated or gathered skirt. Refer to the directions on page 85 for making a pattern for a pleated skirt.

For best results, select a lightweight to medium-weight **fabric** that can be *railroaded*. This will eliminate the need for seams in the rod pocket. The skirt can be seamed in the center if you hide the seam in a pleat or gathers. Two skirt lengths and both rod-pocket pieces can be cut from one width of railroaded 54" (137 cm) decorator fabric, if the skirt is not longer than 16" (40.5 cm).

Mount your mock cornice on a flat, 4½" (11.5 cm) utility rod. If the top treatment is going over an outside-mounted curtain or blind, adjust the mounting brackets to their deepest *projection*. Self-adhesive Velcro strips keep the ends of the sleeve secured to the brackets so the sleeve stays smooth and taut.

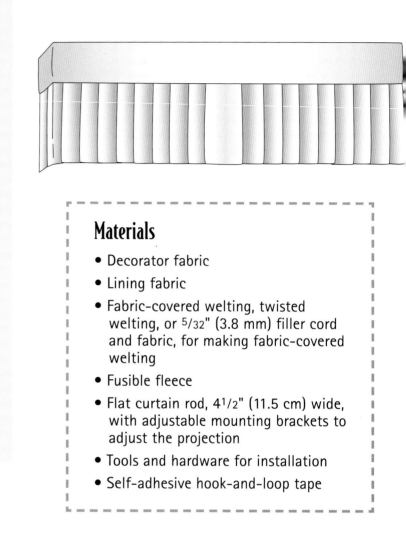

Materials

- Decorator fabric
- Lining fabric
- Fabric-covered welting, twisted welting, or 5/32" (3.8 mm) filler cord and fabric, for making fabric-covered welting
- Fusible fleece
- Flat curtain rod, 4¹/2" (11.5 cm) wide, with adjustable mounting brackets to adjust the projection
- Tools and hardware for installation
- Self-adhesive hook-and-loop tape

Cutting directions

- Cut a strip of decorator fabric for the front of the rod pocket 6" (15 cm) wide, with the length equal to the finished width of the valance (including *returns*) plus 1½" (3.8 cm).

- Cut a strip of decorator fabric for the back of the rod pocket 6" (15 cm) wide, with the length equal to the *cut length* of the front rod-pocket strip plus 1" (2.5 cm).

- Cut a strip of *lining* fabric for the front rod-pocket facing, with the same length and width as the front rod-pocket strip.

- Cut decorator fabric for the skirt, with the length equal to the finished length plus 4½" (11.5 cm).

- For a pleated skirt, make a pattern to determine the cut width, as on page 85, steps 1 to 3. For a gathered skirt, the *cut width* of the skirt is equal to twice the finished width (including returns) plus 1" (2.5 cm).

- Cut lining for the skirt, with the length equal to the finished length of the skirt plus ½" (1.3 cm) and the cut width equal to the cut width of the decorator fabric.

- Cut *bias* fabric strips for fabric-covered welting, as on page 125, step 1.

- Cut a strip of fusible fleece, 5" (12.7 cm) wide, with the length equal to the finished width of the valance (including returns) plus ½" (1.3 cm).

Making a mock cornice– pleated skirt style

1 Center the fusible fleece strip on the wrong side of the front rod-pocket strip; fuse it in place, following the manufacturer's directions.

2 Make fabric-covered welting (page 125) and attach it to the upper and lower edges of the front rod-pocket strip; begin and end the welting ½" (1.3 cm) from the ends of the strip. Or attach purchased welting.

3 Place the front rod pocket over the front rod-pocket facing strip, right sides together, aligning the edges; pin along the lower edge and ends.

4 Stitch a ½" (1.3 cm) seam along the lower edge and ends, using a zipper foot and stitching with the facing side down. Crowd the cording by stitching just inside the previous stitches.

(continued)

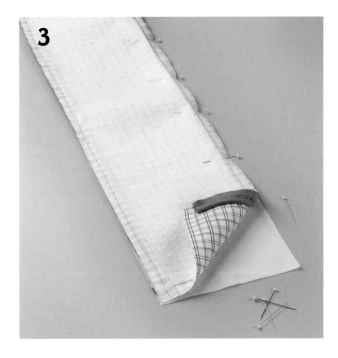

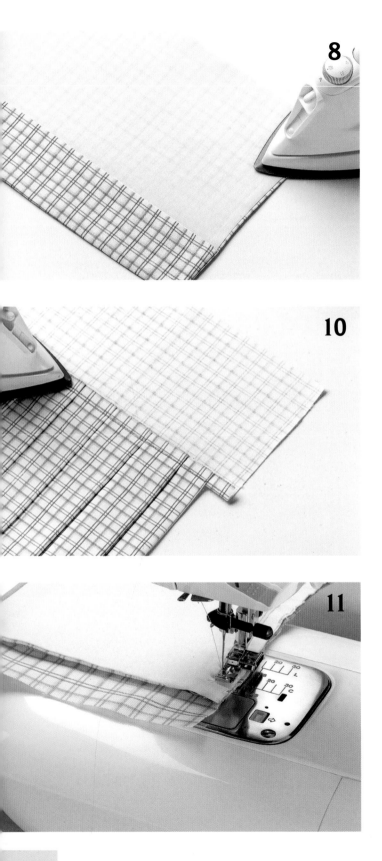

8

10

11

5 Trim the lower corners diagonally. Turn the front rod pocket right side out, and press. Baste the upper edges together within the 1/2" (1.3 cm) seam allowance.

6 Seam the fabric for the skirt, if necessary; repeat for the skirt lining. Pin the skirt and lining, right sides together, along the lower edge. Stitch 2" (5 cm) from the raw edges.

7 Press the 2" (5 cm) hem allowance away from the lining. Pin the skirt to the lining, right sides together, along the sides, aligning the upper edges; the skirt will form a fold even with the lower edge of the hem allowance. Stitch 1/2" (1.3 cm) side seams.

8 Trim the lower corners diagonally. Press the lining side seam allowances toward the lining. Turn the skirt right side out, realigning the upper edges; press. Baste the upper edges together.

9 Make a pattern for the pleated skirt, as on page 83, steps 1 to 3. Lay the skirt faceup on a flat surface; lay the pattern over the upper edge of the skirt, aligning the marked seam lines to the seamed outer edges. Transfer the pattern markings to the skirt. Repeat along the lower edge.

10 Pin the pleats in place along the upper and lower edges of the skirt; press. Baste along the upper edge. Pin the wrong side of the skirt to the right side of the back rod pocket along the lower edge, beginning and ending 1" (2.5 cm) from the end; stitch. Press the seam allowances toward the rod pocket.

11 Pin the back rod pocket to the front rod pocket along the upper edge, right sides together; the ends of the back rod pocket extend 1" (2.5 cm) beyond the ends of the front rod pocket. With the front rod pocket on top, stitch a 1/2" (1.3 cm) seam, using a zipper foot; crowd the welting.

12 Press the seam allowances toward the back rod pocket. Turn under the ends of the back rod-pocket strip ½" (1.3 cm) twice, encasing the ends of the seam allowances; stitch.

13 Turn the skirt and back rod pocket down behind the rod pocket. From the right side, pin the skirt in place along the seam line at the lower edge of the rod pocket, just above the welting.

14 Stitch in the ditch from the right side by stitching in the well of the seam above the welting, using a zipper foot.

15 Insert the curtain rod into the rod pocket. Mount the rod on the brackets. Pull taut toward the returns; secure the returns to the sides of the brackets, using self-adhesive hook-and-loop tape.

Making a mock cornice—gathered skirt style

1 Follow steps 1 to 8 on pages 111 and 112. Zigzag over a cord on the right side of the skirt within the ½" (1.3 cm) seam allowance of the upper edge.

2 Divide the skirt into eighths; pin-mark. Divide the lower edge of the back rod pocket into eighths, beginning and ending 1" (2.5 cm) from the ends. Pin the wrong side of the skirt to the right side of the back rod pocket along the lower edge, matching the pin marks and the raw edges.

3 Pull the gathering cord on the skirt to fit the lower edge of the back rod pocket; pin in place. Stitch ½" (1.3 cm) from the raw edges. Press the seam allowances toward the back rod pocket. Complete the mock cornice, following steps 11 to 15 above.

Soft Cornices

W HILE A PADDED CORNICE is mounted on a box frame, this variation is mounted on a board with side extensions. The look is lighter. A soft cornice can be made as either a single panel of fabric with a shaped lower edge or with overlapping panels. Welting defines the lower edge of the soft cornice and can also trim the upper edge.

Easy angles (opposite)
This soft cornice conforms effortlessly to the angles of the bay window area. Tassel fringe with a decorative heading enhances the lower edge, drawing attention to the gentle curves.

Layers (top)
A tasseled triangle-point hangs freely over a straight plaid panel in this layered soft cornice. Though subtle, the color scheme draws the room together.

Multipurpose (left)
A single-layer soft cornice placed at ceiling level elongates the window area and hides both drapery and shade mechanisms. Pretty tassel fringe defines the edge.

$\mathcal{W}$ hat you need to know

To **design** a soft cornice, first draw it to scale. Tape a full-size paper pattern over the window before beginning the actual project, to check the measurements and proportion.

Use firmly woven decorator **fabric** and back it with fleece for a padded effect. To prevent the shadowing of any seams or overlapped panels, the panels are lined with blackout drapery *lining*.

The **mounting** board for the soft cornice is constructed with legs at the *return* ends to give the treatment added support. The finished width of the soft cornice must be at least 3" (7.5 cm) wider than the outside measurement of the window frame or *undertreatment*; this allows the necessary space for the legs and angle irons.

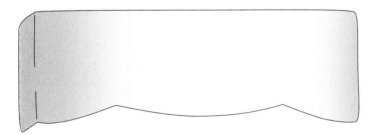

Materials

- Graph paper
- Wide kraft paper or newsprint for making pattern
- Flexible curve or curved ruler
- Decorator fabric for the soft cornice, hem facing, covered mounting board and legs, and dustcover
- Contrasting decorator fabric for the welting
- Filler cord, 1/2" (1.3 cm) thick
- Fusible fleece
- Blackout lining
- Paper-backed fusible adhesive strip, optional
- Glue stick
- Heavy-duty stapler
- Mounting board and side legs
- Four 2 1/2" (6.5 cm) flathead screws for connecting legs to mounting board
- Cardboard stripping
- Self-adhesive hook-and-loop tape
- Tools and hardware for installation

Making the pattern

1 Draw the soft cornice to scale on graph paper. Indicate the finished length at the longest and shortest points, the *projection* of the mounting board, and the finished width of the cornice including returns. Indicate the placement of welting with heavy lines; include 1/2" (1.3 cm) welting at the lower edge and returns in the finished length and width measurements. For a cor-

nice with overlapping panels, draw the shape of
the overlapped panels with dotted lines, and indicate the measurements of each panel.

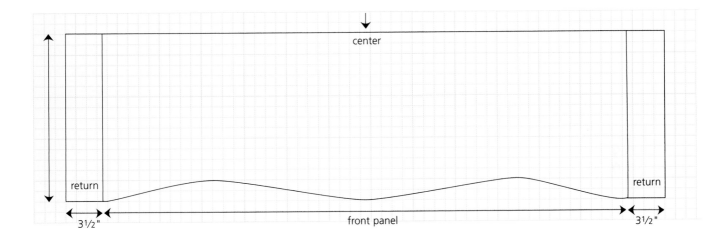

2 Draw a full-size pattern of the soft cornice,
including returns, following your scale drawing.
Use a designing tool, such as a flexible curve or
curved ruler, to draw curved lines along the lower
edge of the pattern. Round the corners. For a cornice
with overlapping panels, draw a pattern for each piece.

3 Cut out the pattern. Do not add seam allowances because the 1/2" (1.3 cm) allowance for
the welting compensates for the seam allowances.
Hang the pattern in the desired location at the top
of the window. Check for accurate measurements
and proportion.

(continued)

Cutting directions

Single panel

- Cut the fabric with the length equal to the finished length at the longest point plus 4" (10 cm).

- The *cut width* of the fabric is equal to the finished width plus twice the projection of the mounting board, plus 4" (10 cm). If the cut width exceeds the fabric width, *railroad* the fabric whenever possible, to avoid any seams. For fabric that cannot be railroaded, cut one fabric width for the center of the panel and seam equal partial widths to each side, matching the pattern in the fabric.

- Cut the fusible fleece to the same size as the decorator fabric.

- Cut the blackout lining to the same size as the decorator fabric.

- Cut one facing strip from the decorator fabric the same width as the lining. To find the cut length of the strip, subtract the shortest point of the cornice from the longest point; then add 3½" (9 cm).

Overlapping panels

- Make a separate pattern for each piece. Cut the fabric, adding a 2" (5 cm) margin around each pattern piece.

- Cut the fusible fleece to the same size as the decorator fabric.

- Cut the blackout lining to the same size as the decorator fabric.

- Cut facing strips for the panels on the return ends only.

Both styles

- From the contrasting fabric, cut *bias* strips, 2½" (6.5 cm) wide to cover the cording for the welting.

- Cut the mounting board. Cut two side legs with the same projection as the mounting board, each 3" (7.5 cm) shorter than the finished length of the soft cornice at the return.

- Cut the fabric for the dustcover 1" (2.5 cm) wider and longer than the width and length of the mounting board.

Making a soft cornice

1 Place the fabric facedown on a pressing surface. Apply fusible fleece to the wrong side of the fabric, following the manufacturer's directions.

2 Place the pattern on the right side of the padded fabric; pin in place within the seam allowances. Cut out the soft cornice along the sides and lower edge; do not trim off the excess fabric at the top.

3 For a one-piece soft cornice or for the return pieces of a multi-piece soft cornice, press under a ½" (1.3 cm) seam allowance along the upper edge of the facing strip. Lay the facing strip over the lining, right side up, matching the lower edge and sides. Stitch close to the fold or secure with paper-backed fusible adhesive strip.

4 Place the pattern facedown over the right side of the lining piece, aligning the lower edges; pin within the seam allowances. Cut out the lining along the sides and lower edge; do not trim off excess fabric at the top. Glue-baste the lower edge of the facing strip to the lining.

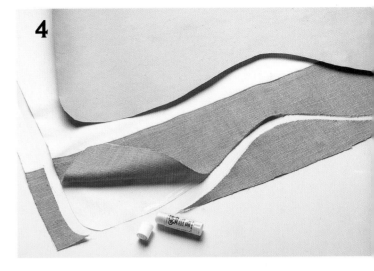

5 Prepare welting as on page 125, steps 1 to 4. Machine-baste the welting to the right side of the padded fabric along the sides and lower edge, matching raw edges and stitching a scant ½" (1.3 cm) from the edges. Clip and ease the welting at the corners and curves.

6 Pin the welted fabric to the lining within the seam allowances, right sides together. Stitch a ½" (1.3 cm) seam along the sides and lower edge, crowding the welting. Clip the seam allowances on the curves; trim the corners. Turn the soft cornice right side out, and press.

7 Measure the desired finished length from the lower edge of the cornice; mark a line on the lining side. Mark a second line 1½" (3.8 cm) above the first line. Cut along the second line through all layers.

(continued)

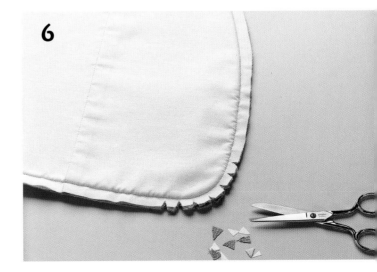

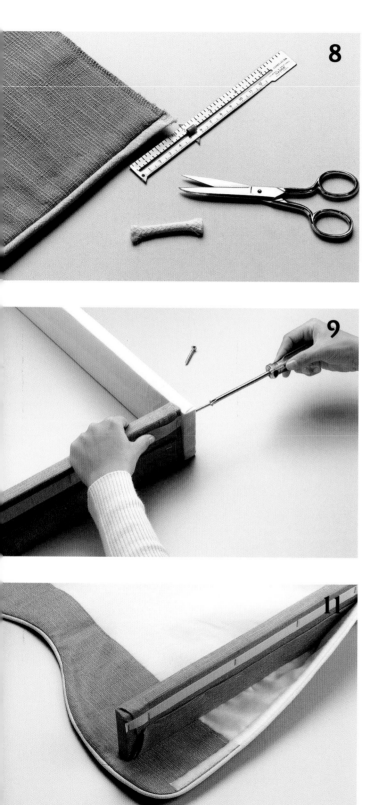

8 Pull out the cord at the ends of the welting; cut off 2" (5 cm) of cording. Pull the seam to draw the cut ends of the cord back into the welting. *Finish* the upper edge by serging or zigzagging through all layers.

9 Cover the mounting board with lining. Cover the legs with decorator fabric. The smooth sides of the legs will face inward. On the outward surface of each leg, staple the hook side of hook-and-loop tape ½" (1.3 cm) from the back edge. Stand the mounting board and legs on edge. Butt the tops of the legs to the underside of the mounting board, outer edges even. Predrill holes for two screws through the mounting board into the end of one leg. Insert the screws. Repeat for the other leg.

10 Cut two strips of loop tape to the same length as the hook tape applied to the legs. Affix the tape to the lining at the return edges of the soft cornice, just inside the welting, with the top of the tape at the marked line.

11 Place the mounting board on the lining side of the soft cornice, with the front edge of the board facedown and the upper edge of the top board even with the marked line. Secure the returns to the legs with the hook-and-loop tape.

12 Support the mounting board on the edge of the work surface. Staple the upper edge of the soft cornice to the top of the mounting board, clipping and overlapping fabric at the corners.

13 Trim ½" (1.3 cm) of cording out of the end of the welting; tuck the fabric into the end, encasing the cord. Staple the welting to the top of the mounting board, along the outer edge, beginning at the back of the board. Allow the welting to overhang the board slightly. Staple to within 3" (7.5 cm) of the opposite end.

14 Cut the welting ½" (1.3 cm) beyond the back edge of the board. Trim ½" (1.3 cm) of cording out of the end. Tuck the fabric into the end, encasing the cord. Finish stapling the welting to the board.

15 On the cornice front, place the dustcover over the welting, with right sides together and raw edges even. Staple cardboard stripping at the front. Fold under the sides of the dustcover even with the sides of the cornice. Insert cardboard stripping into the folds. Pull the fabric to the top of the cornice, and staple in place close to the folds. Fold under the back edge of the dustcover and staple it in place.

16 Secure angle irons to the underside of the mounting board just inside the legs and at 36" (91.5 cm) intervals, using pan-head screws. Hold the soft cornice in its proper position above the window, and mark the screw holes for the angle irons on the wall. Lower the cornice. Remove the angle irons, and attach them to the wall. Mount the cornice by reattaching it to the angle irons on the wall.

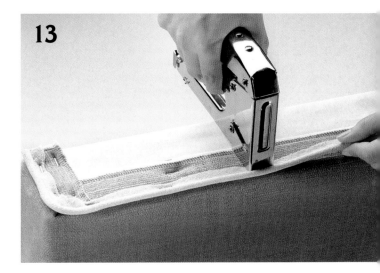

13

Top Treatment Basics

WHATEVER TOP TREATMENT you choose, this basics section will help you plan, sew, and install it. On page 128, you will find definitions of words that are printed in italics.

Choosing and installing hardware

Many top treatments are mounted on rods, poles, or swag holders. Consider both decorative and functional needs when you choose the hardware. Some rods and swag holders are supposed to be covered completely by the fabric, while others have decorative finishes and ornate finials that enhance the treatment. Install the hardware before measuring for the window treatment because the cut length of the fabric depends on the placement of the hardware.

Where do you mount the hardware? Top treatments are mounted either inside or outside the window frame, but usually not directly on the frame. When the top treatment is over curtains or blinds that are mounted outside the frame, you should leave at least 2" (5 cm) of *clearance* between the valance and the *undertreatment* at the front and sides. If the top treatment goes over traversing draperies, leave 3" (7.5 cm) of clearance. When used alone or over a shade or blinds mounted inside the frame, the top treatment can be mounted just outside the frame and have a shallow *projection*.

The correct height for mounting top treatments varies with the style, ceiling height, window size, and overall window treatment. It should be high enough to cover the top of the window frame or any curtains or blinds. If you want to create the illusion that the window is taller than it is, the top treatment can be mounted higher. For good proportion, the length of the top treatment should be about one-fifth the length of the entire treatment. At its shortest point, the top treatment should cover at least 4" to 6" (10 to 15 cm) of window glass to prevent seeing the window frame when you look up.

Window treatment hardware comes with mounting brackets, screws or nails, and installation instructions. Use screws alone if installing through drywall or plaster directly into wall studs. When brackets are between wall studs, support the screws for lightweight treatments with plastic anchors in the correct size for the screws. If the brackets must support a heavy treatment, use plastic toggle anchors or molly bolts in the correct size for the wallboard depth. Nails supplied with hardware should be used only for very lightweight treatments installed directly into wood.

Plastic anchors

1. Mark screw locations on the wall. Drill holes for plastic anchors, using a drill bit slightly smaller than the diameter of the anchor. Tap the anchors into the holes, using a hammer.

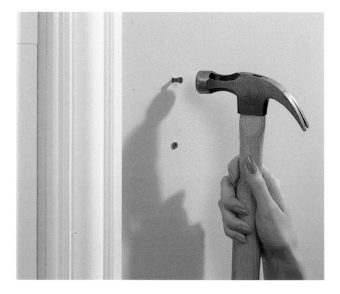

2. Insert a screw through the hole in the bracket and into the installed anchor until it is flush with the wall. Continue to tighten the screw several more turns; the anchor expands in the drywall, preventing it from being pulled out of the wall.

Toggle anchors

1. Mark screw locations on the wall. Drill holes for toggle anchors, using a drill bit slightly smaller than the diameter of the toggle anchor shank.
2. Squeeze the wings of the toggle anchor flat, and push the toggle anchor into the hole; tap it in with a hammer until it is flush with the wall.

3. Insert a screw through the hole in the bracket and into the installed anchor; tighten the screw until it is flush with the wall. The wings spread out and flatten against the back of the drywall.

Molly bolts

1. Mark the screw locations on the wall. Drill holes for the molly bolts, using a drill bit slightly smaller than the diameter of the molly bolt.
2. Tap the molly bolt into the drilled hole, using a hammer; tighten the screw several turns after it is flush with the wall. The molly bolt expands and flattens against the back of the drywall.

3. Remove the screw from the molly bolt; insert the screw through the hole in the bracket and into the installed molly bolt. Screw the bracket securely in place.

Mounting boards

Many valances are mounted on boards instead of window hardware. The mounting board is covered with extra valance fabric, much as you would wrap a gift box, but secured with staples instead of tape. Then the valance is stapled to the board.

The size of the mounting board depends on whether the valance will be mounted inside or outside the window frame and whether it will be used alone or over another treatment. Stock pine lumber is often the best choice because it is inexpensive, lightweight, and only needs to be cut to the right length. Keep in mind that the actual measurement of stock lumber differs from the nominal measurement. A 1 × 2 board is really 3/4" × 1 1/2" (2 × 3.8 cm), a 1 × 4 board is 3/4" × 3 1/2" (2 × 9 cm), a 1 × 6 board is 3/4" × 5 1/2" (2 × 14 cm), and a 1 × 8 board is 3/4" × 7 1/4" (2 × 18.7 cm).

(continued)

123

For an inside-mounted valance, the depth of the window frame must be at least 1½" (3.8 cm) to accommodate a 1 × 2 mounting board. Cut the board ½" (1.3 cm) shorter than the inside measurement of the frame so it will still fit after being covered with fabric. Choose the mounting board width for outside-mounted valances following the general guidelines for clearance on page 122.

Install mounting boards and cornice boards using angle irons that are more than one-half the projection of the board. You will need one at each end and others spaced about 36" (91.5 cm) apart.

Working with decorator fabric

Decorator fabrics intended for window treatments have characteristics not found in fashion fabrics. They are more durable and have often been treated to resist stains. When cleaning is necessary, most decorator fabrics must be dry-cleaned to avoid shrinkage. Care information is given on the fabric identification label, found on the bolt or tube.

Decorator fabrics should be preshrunk to ensure they won't shrink during construction or the first time they are cleaned. To do this, roll out the fabric and slowly hover a steam iron back and forth just above the surface.

To make sure the valance will hang correctly, the fabric lengths must be cut on-grain. Tightly woven fabrics that do not need to be matched at the seams can be cut perpendicular to the selvages, using a carpenter's square as a guide for marking

the cutting line. For lightweight and loosely woven fabrics, it is better to pull a thread along the *crosswise grain* and cut along the pulled thread.

Matching patterns

Patterned decorator fabrics are designed to match at the seams. Cuts are made across the fabric, from selvage to selvage, following the *pattern repeat* rather than the fabric grain, so it is very important to purchase fabric that is printed on-grain. The pattern repeat is the lengthwise distance from one distinctive point in the design, such as the tip of a petal in a floral pattern, to the same point in the next repeat of the design. Some patterned fabrics have pattern repeat markings printed on the selvages.

Extra yardage is usually needed so you can match the pattern. After finding the *cut length* for the main pieces of a valance, round this measurement up to the next number divisible by the size of the pattern repeat to determine the revised cut length. To have the design match from one panel to the next, each panel must be cut at exactly the same point of the pattern repeat.

1. Cut the fabric pieces to the revised cut length, allowing extra for matching the print. Place two fabric pieces right sides together, aligning the selvages. Fold back the upper selvage until the pattern matches. Adjust the top layer slightly up or down so the pattern lines up exactly. Press the fold line.

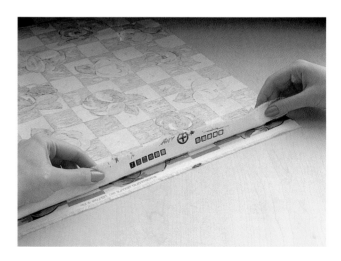

2. Unfold the pressed selvage and pin the layers together, in the fold line. Turn the fabric over and check the match from the right side. Make any necessary adjustments.

3 Re-pin the fabric so the pins are perpendicular to the fold line; stitch on the fold line. Trim away the selvages, cutting the seam allowances to ½" (1.3 cm). *Finish* the seam allowances, if necessary.

4. Repeat steps 2 to 4 for all the pieces in the panel. Trim the entire panel to the necessary cut length.

Decorative trims

Welting, fringes, and other decorative accents dramatically change the appearance of top treatments. They give rich style and grace to valances and cornices by accenting design lines and adding color and textural interest.

Fabric-covered welting

Welting adds an attractive emphasis to seam lines and edges of certain valances. In a gathered pickup valance (page 70), for instance, welting defines the lower edge and stiffens it for better shaping. Ready-to-sew fabric-covered cording is available in a limited selection of decorator colors and thicknesses.

You can cover filler cord with the fabric of your choice for a perfect match to your window treatment. To make fabric-covered welting, fabric strips are cut on the *bias* so the welting will be more flexible around curves and corners. Cut bias strips as wide as the circumference of the filler cord plus 1" (2.5 cm).

1. Fold the fabric diagonally so the selvage is parallel to the *crosswise grain*; cut on the fold. Measuring from this cut edge, cut bias strips of the necessary width, cutting the ends at 45-degree angles on the straight grain.

2. Seam the strips together as necessary; press the seam allowances open. Cut the end of the strip straight across. Center the filler cord on the wrong side of the strip, with the end of the cord 1" (2.5 cm) from the end of the strip. Fold the end of the strip over the cording.

3. Fold the fabric strip around the cording, wrong sides together, matching the raw edges and encasing the cording.

4. Machine-baste close to the cording, using a zipper foot.

5. Stitch the welting to the right side of the valance, as indicated in the project instructions, matching raw edges and stitching over the basting stitches. Stop stitching 5" (12.7 cm) from where you want the welting to stop.

(continued)

6. Cut the welting 1" (2.5 cm) beyond the desired end point. Remove the basting stitches from the end of the welting, and cut the cord even with the desired end point.

7. Fold the end of the bias strip over the cord, encasing the cut end. Finish stitching the welting to the valance fabric.

Twisted cord welting

Twisted cord welting, an ornate alternative to fabric-covered welting, is available in a variety of styles and colors. A welt tape, or lip, is attached to decorative cord for sewing into a seam. From the right side of the welting, the inner edge of the tape in not visible. Be sure to attach the welting with the right side facing out.

1. Pin the welting to the valance fabric, right sides together, with the cord ½" (1.3 cm) from the raw edge of the fabric and the ends extending 1" (2.5 cm) beyond the starting and stopping points.
2. Remove the stitching from the welting tape for about 1½" (3.8 cm) at the ends.
3. Turn the welting tape into the seam allowance and pin or tape it in place. Turn the untwisted cords into the seam allowance, following the pattern of the twist and flattening them as much as possible.

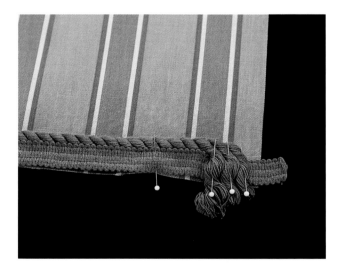

4. Stitch the welting to the fabric ½" (1.3 cm) from the raw edge, using a zipper foot and crowding the cord. Trim the ends of the cord.

Decorator fringes

Fringes come in a wide range of styles and colors, many with coordinating braids and tassels. Fringes that have a decorative *heading* should be sewn, glued, or fused onto the right side of the valance. Those that have a plain heading should be sewn into a seam, encasing the heading so only the fringe is exposed. Consider the length of the fringe when you plan your top treatment. While fringe offers a dramatic look, it also affects the finished length of the valance.

In the photograph, numbers identify the following types of fringe:

Brush fringe (1) is a dense row of threads all cut to the same length. When you buy it in the store, the cut ends of the threads are secured with a chain stitch, which should be left in until you complete the project. After pulling out the chain stitch, fluff out the fringe by steaming and gentle brushing. Cut fringe has a decorative heading and is similar to brush fringe but not usually as dense. The threads are often multicolored.

Loop fringe (2) is made with a decorative heading. The fringe is a series of overlapping looped threads that can be the same or different lengths.

Tassel fringe (3) is a continuous row of miniature tassels attached to a decorative heading.

Ball fringe (4) is a continuous row of pom-poms hanging from a plain heading. Similar to the popular craft trim, decorator ball fringe is more ornate.

Bullion fringe (5) is a row of twisted cords attached to a decorative heading. Styles vary in length and weight with single-color or multicolored cords. Cotton bullion fringe is casual, while rayon or acetate bullion fringes are very elegant.

Beaded fringes (6) are very chic. They are available in many styles; some resemble cut, loop, or ball fringes but are made with hundreds of beads in all sorts of shapes, sizes, and colors.

Here are some tips for attaching fringe:

- Apply liquid fray preventer liberally to the area of the heading that will be cut; allow it to dry completely before cutting the fringe.

- To attach fringe with a decorative heading, pin or glue-baste the fringe in the desired location on the right side of the finished window treatment, turning under ¾" (2 cm) at the ends of the heading. Straight-stitch along the top and bottom of the heading.

- Instead of stitching, fuse the heading to the fabric, using paper-backed fusible adhesive tape.

- Glue the heading in place with fabric glue.

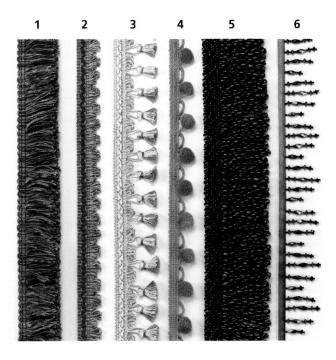

Terms to Know

Bias. Any diagonal line intersecting the lengthwise and crosswise grains of fabric. While woven fabric is very stable on the lengthwise and crosswise grains, it has considerable stretch on the bias.

Clearance. The distance between the back of the rod or valance and the wall or undertreatment, measured at the front and sides. There must be enough clearance so the layers of the window treatment do not interfere with each other.

Crosswise grain. On woven fabrics, the crosswise grain is perpendicular to the selvages. Fabric has slight "give" in the crosswise grain.

Cut length. The total length at which fabric pieces should be cut for the valance. It includes allowances for any hems, headings, rod pockets, and ease.

Cut width. The total width the fabric should be cut. If more than one width of fabric is needed, the cut width refers to the entire panel after seams are sewn, including allowances for any side hems.

Finish. To improve the durability of a seam, the raw edges are secured with stitches that prevent them from fraying. This can be done with zigzag stitches that wrap over the edge or with serging.

Fullness. The finished width of a valance compared to the length of the rod or mounting board. For example, two times fullness means that the width of the fabric is two times the length of the rod.

Heading. The portion at the top of a rod-pocket valance that forms a ruffle when the valance is on the rod. The depth of the heading is the distance from the finished upper edge to the top stitching line for the rod pocket.

Interlining. A layer of fabric (usually drapery lining) encased between the top fabric and the lining to prevent light from shining through or to add body to the treatment.

Lengthwise grain. On woven fabrics, the lengthwise grain runs parallel to the selvages. Fabrics are generally stronger along the lengthwise grain.

Lined-to-the-edge. A fabric panel backed with lining that is cut to the exact same size. The two pieces are joined together by a seam around the edge.

Lining. A fabric backing sewn to the face fabric to provide extra body, protection from sunlight, and support for side hems.

On-grain. When the lengthwise and crosswise yarns in woven fabric are perfectly aligned. If the crosswise grain is not perfectly perpendicular to the lengthwise grain as the fabric is printed, it will be impossible to match up the pattern or to have a treatment that hangs evenly with straight-cut lower edges.

Pattern repeat. The lengthwise distance from one distinctive point in the fabric pattern, such as the tip of a particular petal in a floral pattern, to the same point in the next pattern design.

Projection. The distance a rod or mounting board stands out from the wall.

Railroading. Normally the lengthwise grain of the fabric runs vertically in a window treatment. Since decorator fabric is usually 54" (137 cm) wide, treatments that are wider than this must have vertical seams joining additional widths of fabric. Railroading means the fabric is turned sideways, so the lengthwise grain runs horizontally. The full width can then be cut in one piece, eliminating the need for any seams.

Return. The portion of the top treatment that extends from the end of the rod or mounting board to the wall, blocking the side light and view.

Self-lined. A fabric panel lined-to-the-edge with the same fabric. Rather than cutting two pieces and sewing them together, one double-length piece is cut, folded right sides together, and stitched on the remaining three sides, so one edge will have a fold instead of a seam.

Undertreatment. A window treatment—curtains, draperies, blinds, or a shade—installed under the top treatment, either inside or outside the window frame. The undertreatment is mounted on its own hardware, independent of the top treatment.